D0356479

PRIORITY LEADERSHIP

Generating School and District Improvement through Systemic Change

Robert T. Hess and James W. Robinson

Rowman & Littlefield Education
Lanham • New York • Toronto • Oxford
2006

Published in the United States of America
by Rowman & Littlefield Education
A Division of Rowman & Littlefield Publishers, Inc.
A wholly owned subsidiary of The Rowman & Littlefield Publishing Group,
Inc.
4501 Forbes Boulevard, Suite 200, Lanham, Maryland 20706
www.rowmaneducation.com

PO Box 317
Oxford
OX2 9RU, UK

Copyright © 2006 by Robert T. Hess and James W. Robinson

British Library Cataloguing in Publication Information Available

Library of Congress Cataloging-in-Publication Data

Hess, Robert T. (Robert Thomas), 1962–
  Priority leadership : generating school and district improvement through
systemic change / Robert T. Hess and James W. Robinson.
      p. cm.
  Includes bibliographical references.
  ISBN-13: 978-1-57886-437-9 (cloth : alk. paper)
  ISBN-10: 1-57886-437-2 (cloth : alk. paper)
  ISBN-13: 978-1-57886-438-6 (pbk. : alk. paper)
  ISBN-10: 1-57886-438-0 (pbk. : alk. paper)
   1. School improvement programs—United States. 2. Educational
leadership—United States. 3. Educational change—United States. I.
Robinson, James Warren, 1948– II. Title.
LB2822.82.H493 2006
371.2—dc22   2005037856

∞™ The paper used in this publication meets the minimum requirements of
American National Standard for Information Sciences—Permanence of Paper
for Printed Library Materials, ANSI/NISO Z39.48-1992.
Manufactured in the United States of America.

Leading Systemic School Improvement Series

...helping change leaders transform entire school systems

This Rowman & Littlefield Education series provides change leaders in school districts with a collection of books written by prominent authors with an interest in creating and sustaining whole-district school improvement. It features young, relatively unpublished authors with brilliant ideas, as well as authors who are cross-disciplinary thinkers.

Whether an author is prominent or relatively unpublished, the key criterion for a book's inclusion in this series is that it must address an aspect of creating and sustaining systemic school improvement. For example, books from members of the business world, developmental psychology, and organizational development are good candidates as long as they focus on creating and sustaining whole-system change in school district settings; books about building-level curriculum reform, instructional methodologies, and team communication, although interesting and helpful, are not appropriate for the series unless they discuss how these ideas can be used to create whole-district improvement.

Since the series is for practitioners, highly theoretical or research-reporting books aren't included. Instead, the series provides an artful blend of theory and practice—in other words, books based on theory and research but written in plain, easy-to-read language. Ideally, theory and research are artfully woven into practical descriptions of how to create and sustain systemic school improvement. The series is subdivided into three categories:

Why Systemic School Improvement Is Needed and Why It's Important. This is the *why*. Possible topics within this category include the history of systemic school improvement; the underlying philosophy of systemic school improvement; how systemic school improvement is different from school-based improvement; and the driving forces of standards, assessments, and accountability and why systemic improvement can respond effectively to these forces.

The Desirable Outcomes of Systemic School Improvement. This is the *what*. Possible topics within this category include comprehensive school reform models scaled up to create whole-district improvement; strategic alignment; creating a high-performance school system; redesigning a school system as a learning organization; unlearning and learning mental models; and creating an organization design flexible and agile enough to respond quickly to unanticipated events in the outside world.

How to Create and Sustain Systemic School Improvement. This is the *how*. Possible topics within this category include methods for redesigning entire school systems; tools for navigating complex change; ideas from the "new sciences" for creating systemic change; leadership methods for creating systemic change; evaluating the process and outcomes of systemic school improvement; and financing systemic school improvement.

The series editor, Dr. Francis M. Duffy, can be reached at 301-854-9800 or fmduffy@earthlink.net.

Leading Systemic School Improvement Series

Edited by Francis M. Duffy

For Jeanne . . .

Who has her priorities straight.

—Rob

For Chris . . .

Our partnership enables our leadership.

—Jim

CONTENTS

ACKNOWLEDGMENTS

A book of this nature is not created in a vacuum. We owe a great deal to the many colleagues with whom we interacted and worked side by side over a period of several years while developing the concepts that went into this book. There were many days and times of lively discussion that continually refined and improved the work again and again.

Because of its ongoing nature, a project of this kind is never really finished. It just keeps getting refined and sharpened over time, and then it is due. We can see ways to improve the project, and should *Priority Leadership* find its way into the leadership field, there will undoubtedly be subsequent editions as the concepts get applied and tried in various settings.

A special thanks goes to Steve Kelley, Director of Student Achievement in Lebanon, Oregon, whose ideas and writing helped shape some sections of the work. Additional recognition goes to the follow educators who edited various chapters and provided meaningful feedback during the revision process: Olga Acuna, Brian Bray, Tonya Cairo, Pam Edens, Gary Lewis, Jim Mangan, Jane Paxson, Debbie Price, Erika Pinkerton, Bob Vian, and Matthew Wilding. We are indebted to the helpful feedback these people provided. We are also grateful to Justin Howard of Cybermerge.com, who created the SAS graphic.

We would like to thank Dr. Tom Koerner, the editor-in-chief at Rowman & Littlefield Education, who believed in this project from the beginning, and Dr. Francis Duffy, who gave us helpful feedback about systemic change and felt this book was worthy to be included in his school leadership series.

We would also like to thank all of the hardworking educators we have come to know over the years. It is their untiring dedication to continuous improvement that sparks ideas and books of this nature. It is our hope that this book will provide another tool to help facilitate the kind of wholesale systemic change needed in public education today.

FOREWORD

Did you hear the story about a dog that walked into a butcher shop with a wallet in its mouth? I didn't think so. Let me tell it to you.

A dog walked into a butcher shop with a wallet in its mouth. The butcher was shocked by this and asked the dog, "Can I help you?" The dog replied, "Ruff." The butcher asked, "Do you want to buy some meat?" The dog replied, "Ruff." The butcher, who was astonished by the dog's intelligence, asked, "Well, what kind would you like?"

The dog started looking in the meat case and soon she spotted a succulent roast in the corner of the case. She pointed her nose at it and replied, "Ruff." And the butcher asked, "Well, how much would you like?" And the dog replied, "Ruff, ruff." The butcher asked, "Two pounds?" And the dog replied, "Ruff." Well, the butcher now was thoroughly impressed by the dog's intelligence.

The butcher sliced two pounds of meat, wrapped it up and put it in a brown paper sack. Then he picked up the dog's wallet and you'll never guess what was inside that wallet. That's right—the exact amount of money that dog needed to pay for two pounds of roast. So, the butcher took out the money and put the wallet in the brown paper sack. The dog picked up the sack and left.

The butcher really wanted to find out where this dog lived. So, he closed up the shop and followed the dog down the street to a local apartment building. The dog went in. The butcher followed and found a hiding place. The dog went up to one of the doors and started barking and scratching at the door.

Soon a man came to the door and started to yell and scream at the poor dog. Well, the butcher couldn't take this any more so he came out from his hiding place and walked up to the man and said, "Mister, you can't talk to this dog like that. She is the smartest dog I have ever seen in my life!" The man looked at the butcher, looked at the dog, and then looked at the butcher and said, "Smart—you think this dog's smart—this is the third time this week she's forgotten her keys!"

You see, sometimes no matter how much you do it's just not enough!

And when it comes to improving the quality of education in school districts, educators I meet from all over the country tell me that sometimes it feels like no matter how much they do it's just not enough. You know what I mean.

- You develop a new curriculum and no one uses it; or they use it inappropriately.
- Your superintendent launches a major change agenda and 2.8 years later he or she quits or is fired and the new superintendent launches a new change agenda that sweeps out previous improvements.
- You work hard to develop positive relationships with key community members and parents and some of them write letters to the editor of your local newspaper complaining that you are "not doing enough."
- Your students' performances on mandatory state assessments are improving but your state department of education tells you that "it's not enough."

I used to think that problems like the ones listed above, and others not mentioned, were the fault of individuals. But after I started studying how school districts function as systems I learned something very important. *I learned that I was wrong.* Problems like these often are not the fault of individuals. Quality improvement experts like W. Edwards Deming (1986) have proclaimed for years that 80–85 percent of the time problems like the ones I just listed are caused by system failures, not by individuals;

therefore, efforts to improve education in school districts must focus on system-wide improvement. And this is the need to which Robert Hess and James Robinson's book responds. By the time you finish reading their book you will be empowered to transform your whole school system.

FOUR BELIEFS ABOUT YOUR SCHOOL SYSTEM

To become empowered to lead the transformation of your entire school system you will need to embrace four beliefs—beliefs that I learned from conversations with people like you: teachers, building administrators, superintendents, school board members, and policymakers. The four beliefs are:

1. Within the context of the No Child Left Behind Act, your system is at risk of failing you.
2. Your current approach to improving your system is insufficient (it's not enough).
3. There must be another way to improve your system.
4. No matter what that other way is, your colleagues will object to it.

Let's explore each belief in turn.

Belief 1: Your system is at risk of failing you. The No Child Left Behind Act has requirements that put a large percentage of America's districts at risk of failing. Typically, efforts to improve districts in response to NCLB are not systemic. One of the key reasons school systems fail educators is that they are, in fact, systems; but they are not improved as systems. Russell Ackoff (1999) warns us clearly about why systems must be managed as systems. He says " . . . a system is a whole entity that cannot be divided into individual parts without loss of its essential properties or functions." Yet, isn't this exactly what educators often do in their school districts? Don't they disassemble their systems into their component parts—individual schools and programs—and then manage those schools and programs under the banner of school-based management?

Please don't misunderstand me. School-based management is important and it must continue, but by itself it is an insufficient strategy for managing the performance of an entire school system—it's simply not enough. If your district is practicing school-based management and not practicing system-wide management, then your system is failing you. Let me make this point a bit differently with an analogy.

Imagine a fleet of ships setting sail from Norfolk, Virginia, heading for Spain. In the middle of the fleet is an aircraft carrier with an admiral on board. The carrier is surrounded by several destroyers and cruisers and a couple of submarines underwater. About 100 miles out to sea, the admiral gets on the radio to all of his ship's captains and says, "Okay, fellas, it's every ship for itself now. See you in Madrid in 10 days. Good luck."

Can you imagine that happening? Can you imagine the effect that announcement would have on the power of that fleet and on the effectiveness of the individual ships. Yes, each individual ship has its own captain and each ship has its own crew. But the power and effectiveness of that fleet is in its ability to sail together as a unit of one.

In much the same way, a school system is like that fleet. Yes, each individual school has its own principal and its own faculty. Yes, each individual school sails under the power of school-based management. But the effectiveness of a school system is found in its ability to perform as a unit of one. If individual schools in your system are sailing alone without being strategically aligned with a system-wide strategic framework, your system is failing you.

Belief 2: Your current approach to improving your system is insufficient. Lew Rhodes is the former assistant executive director of the Association for Supervision and Curriculum Development and the former assistant director of American Association of School Administrators. He's also a friend of mine.

Lew and I were having coffee one day at our local Starbucks discussing why whole-system change is necessary. At one point in the conversation, Lew asked a rhetorical question, "If school-based improvement is so effective, why is it that after more than 30 years of using it so little has changed?" Of course, both Lew and I knew the answer. School-based improvement is important. It is necessary. It must continue. But by itself it is not enough—it's insufficient for improving an entire system. You may be wondering why. It is an insufficient approach because a school district is a system and school-based improvement is non-systemic.

All systems have three key components (Duffy 2002, 2003, 2004a, 2004b): an external environment, core and supporting work processes, and an internal social "architecture" (a.k.a., work environment). The three major components of a school district as a system create three change paths that must be followed simultaneously to improve student, faculty and staff, and whole-system learning. These paths are: Path 1—improve the district's relationship with the external environment; Path 2—improve the district's core and supporting work processes; and Path 3—improve the district's internal social architecture. In the field of organization development this three path approach to improvement is called "joint optimization" (Cummings and Worley, 2001).

Here's another way of thinking about the three paths to improvement. Your district might have a fabulous instructional program and maybe you've adopted a research-proven instructional methodology. But what if your teachers are demotivated and demoralized because of an ineffective internal social architecture? Demotivated and demoralized teachers will not use a fabulous program in remarkable ways. So, you must improve your internal social architecture (Path 3) to improve motivation and job satisfaction.

Maybe your district has highly motivated teachers but your instructional program is not producing desired results (Path 2—core work). If your instructional program has weaknesses in it, highly motivated teachers cannot succeed. Or maybe you have highly motivated teachers and a truly effective instructional program, but, for example, the exteriors of your buildings are unkempt, your bus transportation system doesn't work well, and the food served in your cafeteria is unsatisfying to the students (Path 2—supporting work). Problems in the supporting work area can reduce the overall effectiveness of your system. So, you need to improve the core and supporting work processes.

What if you have highly motivated teachers and staff, your core and supporting work processes are superior, but you don't have good relationships with key stakeholders in your community (Path 1)? If your district doesn't have good relationships with its environment, then no matter how effective your district is those key stakeholders will continue to complain that you are "not doing enough."

You need to make and sustain changes along all three paths if you want to create unparalleled opportunities to improve student, faculty and staff, and whole-system learning. If your current approach to improving your system does not follow these three paths simultaneously that approach is insufficient. Hess and Robinson's approach to creating and sustaining whole-system change will help you move along those three change paths.

Belief 3: There must be another way to improve our system. If your system is in danger of failing you and if your current approach to improving your system is insufficient, you may be wondering if there is another way to improve your system. There is. It's called "whole-system improvement" or "systemic change."[1]

Hess and Robinson's book provides you with a model for creating and sustaining whole-system change in your district using principles like the ones I outlined above. Their book draws from different related literatures to synthesize an approach to systemic change they call "priority leadership." It's a powerful approach for creating systemic change.

Belief 4: No matter what that other way to improve your district, some of your colleagues will object to it. Every time I speak to an audience about creating and sustaining whole-system change in school districts I predictably hear four key objections to the idea. The objections take the form of "yes, buts." Here are the three common objections:

- Yes, this is a good idea; but who else is doing this?
- Yes, this is a good idea; but how do we pay for it?
- Yes, this is a good idea; but how can we stop doing what we're doing to engage in this kind of change?

If you want to use Hess and Robinson's model for creating and sustaining whole-system change, then you need to anticipate these objections. Then, you must provide answers to the objections before they are voiced. This anticipatory action will help neutralize the power of the objections and help you build political support for change.

In my opinion, Hess and Robinson's book is a wonderful addition to the literature on how to create and sustain whole-system change in school districts. I believe it will be useful to those of you who are leading or aspire to lead whole-system change in your districts.

Francis M. Duffy
Highland, Maryland

---

1. I often see the term "systematic change" used instead of "systemic change." There is an important difference between the terms "systematic" and "systemic." "Systematic" refers to a process that is organized, structured, and well-planned. "Systemic" refers to a process that focuses on the whole system, not just pieces of it. Systemic change should be systematic, but systematic change is not always systemic.

REFERENCES

Ackoff, R. L. 1999. *Re-creating the Corporation: A Design of Organizations for the 21st Century.* New York: Oxford University Press.

Cummings, T. G. and Worley, C. G. 2001. *Organization Development and Change.* 7th ed. Cincinnati, Ohio: South-Western College Publishing.

Deming, W. E. 1986. *Out of the Crisis.* Cambridge: Massachusetts Institute of Technology, Center for Advanced Engineering Study.

Duffy, F. M. 2002. *Step-Up-To-Excellence: An Innovative Approach to Managing and Rewarding Performance in School Systems.* Lanham, Md.: Scarecrow Press.

Duffy, F. M. 2003. *Courage, Passion, and Vision: A Superintendent's Guide to Leading Systemic School Improvement.* Lanham, Md.: Scarecrow Press and the American Association of School Administrators.

Duffy, F. M. 2004a. "Navigating Whole-System Change: Eight Principles for Moving an Organization Upward in Times of Unpredictability." *The School Administrator* 61, no. 1: 22–25.

Duffy, F. M. 2004b. *Moving Upward Together: Creating Strategic Alignment to Sustain Systemic School Improvement.* Leading Systemic School Improvement 1. Lanham, Md.: Scarecrow Press.

INTRODUCTION

This book is not only about navigating the tumultuous waves of change in education but about learning how to successfully implement *systemic* change. Systemic change is the understanding that the parts are always connected to the whole, and meaningful improvement does not happen by tinkering with the parts. It only occurs when we address the system as a whole. A school district is made up of many parts: individual buildings, food service, transportation, curriculum, etc. Individual schools have many parts as well. This book doesn't show you what to do as much as teaches you what *to be*, and as you embrace the concepts of priority leadership, you will think and act differently. As a result, you will approach improvement from a systems perspective. You will begin to see connections between departments and focus on the whole instead of the pieces. The result will be breakthrough performance. This book is for leaders who embrace change, followers who resist it, and anyone who wants to get more done at work.

Although the target audience is educators, the book draws examples from other fields that live and die on results—the worlds of business and sports. Education has been shifting to a results-oriented culture over the last 10 years, and operating in this new environment will require a new leadership skill set. Change theory is not static. It is systemic. There should always be new books about change that view improvement as a systems effort. We feel this one will be an important link in change theory as applied to education that leaders can use to in their migration to a results-orientated public school system.

Improvement means change. If you work in a for-profit business, your survival is dependent upon improvement. If you work in a school, the wheels of reform and accountability roll a lot more slowly, but they are catching up. The authors of *Priority Leadership* are long time supporters of public education, but whether we like to admit it or not, we can read the writing on the wall. The public education monopoly is over. With the advent of charter schools, private schools, home schools, alternative schools, and the booming growth of the Internet, public schools in many communities have moved from the only option to one of many. In the days to come, public schools must demonstrate improvement, and improvement means ongoing change in a positive direction that can be verified by measurable results. Schools and districts that languish in the status quo hoping that the "good ol' days" of complete public trust will return may find themselves on the bottom of AYP lists or worse yet: replaced by for-profits, charters, or online alternatives.

Change is happening all around us. Harvard educator and reformer Samuel Betances states, "Change is inevitable. Growth is optional" (2002). Leadership is about systemic change—not only managing it, but using it as a lever for improvement.

In the world of leadership there are two types of organizations: non-profit (social sector) and profit (business sector). It is easier to be successful in the business sector as an agent of change than in the social sector. Many leaders who move from the social sector to business sector are successful. Few go the other way. The reason is simple. In the world of non-profits, leaders have a great deal of legislative power and very little authoritative power. They have to convince people to change. In the profit world leaders have more authoritative power. They tell people to change, and if they don't, they find someone else who will.

This is one of the many reasons that meaningful change is so rare in public schools today. Most school leaders don't stay in one place long enough to build up the trust necessary to convince anybody to change, or they do not have the courage to rock the status quo for very long. Superintendents know if they push too hard, the legislative powers that surround them will be their undoing. There is a deep need to please the people in order to survive. There is a great deal of pressure not to challenge the status quo. A bad report from one district can make it nearly impossible to land another job. This book is about creating meaningful, enduring, and effective systemic change in schools in spite of these pressures. To illustrate our points in the world of education, we have borrowed from both business and sports because the leadership principles presented are universal and can be applied to any setting.

Although we target educators, the lessons offered carry over to the world of business as well. The business sector is changing every day and is becoming increasingly complex. We have a smarter workforce that asks questions and won't always settle for the company line. The leaders of tomorrow's companies will need to know how to lead without power—which is what leaders in the social sector do everyday (Hesselbein 2004) For this reason, the principles presented in this book become even more valuable with applications beyond the realm of schools and other non-profits.

Priority Leadership not only shows what actions and attitudes leaders should take, but what pitfalls to avoid. Each chapter addresses hindrances to change and hallways for improvement. A central theme of the book is not only why systemic change is good, but also why it should be pursued and embraced. It is a practical book that will put into the hands of educators a blue print for positive change that will lead to measurable improvement.

Each of the 10 chapters is presented as a continuum of growth. Leadership is complex and continuums are an effective way to demonstrate complexity that emphasizes growth over time.

CHAPTER 1: FROM PLANNING TO VISION

Leadership is not about making plans. It is about achieving results. Excessive and detailed plans can easily become a distraction to achieving meaningful results, because so much time and energy is put into the plans, it becomes time lost from doing the actual work. Planning is a threat to systemic change. Most creative innovations happen when people deviate from the plan.

Plans seldom generate results. Vision generates results. Effective leaders bringing positive, meaningful change to their organizations have vision. It is vision that drives systemic change, not plans. Plans can and will get in the way of meaningful change because there is not a pre-scribed path to breakthrough improvement. Plans, by definition, are prescribed paths.

CHAPTER 2: FROM GOALS TO PRIORITIES

At first glance, the difference between goal setting and priorities is just semantics, but in reality they are fundamentally different. Understand-ing the difference is a major step in moving toward a systemic change agenda that will lead to improvement. Goals are short-term destinations. They are achievable objectives. Priorities are a state of being—the mak-ings of a journey that requires commitment. Goal setting is manage-ment. Priorities are leadership. Management maintains the status quo while leadership generates improvement via change. Systemic change does not come through goal setting; it is birthed via the determined ap-plication of priorities.

CHAPTER 3: FROM POLICY TO OPPORTUNITY

Stifled, fearful organizations are governed by policy. Leaner, result-oriented organizations are governed by priority, which allows them the freedom to pursue *targets of opportunity* when they arise. A sys-tem that is ruled by priorities or principles is nimble and enables leaders to spend less time planning how to protect the status quo via policy and more time on innovations that present themselves as tar-gets of opportunity.

Most events that result in great achievement for companies and cor-porations are not the offspring of determined planning. Usually they are the result of a disciplined pursuit of the right opportunities that pre-sented themselves somewhere along the way. Being ready to pursue tar-gets of opportunity opens up the door to innovation, and innovation is a precursor to effective change. They expand the field of vision.

Governance by policy, on the other hand, prevents innovation by constantly reinforcing the most dangerous and preventive change statement of all time: "We've never done it that way before." When it comes to developing an improvement-oriented culture, that statement in itself should be the number one reason to do *something different*. Organizations that are on the lookout for and pursue targets of opportunity have a high tolerance for risk-taking and making mistakes, but even more importantly, unearth improvements and innovations that never would have been discovered otherwise.

CHAPTER 4: FROM PROBLEM-SOLVING TO CAPACITY-BUILDING

Leaders become leaders because they want to help people, and many times they help people by solving their problems—being the hero. Unfortunately, stepping in to solve problems does not build capacity in followers. It enables the status quo. People do not learn new ways of thinking and working when their problems are solved for them. The art of delegation is a learned skill. Delegating leadership roles to others and then stepping back and giving them authority to act is the most effective way to build capacity.

The more staff members become reliant on themselves and each other to solve problems, the more intrinsic and disciplined a team becomes. Almost all effective innovations that create systemic change stem from workers increasing capacity through intrinsic motivation and spreading that innovation to others.

CHAPTER 5: FROM ISOLATION AND FEAR OF SEPARATION TO RELATIONSHIPS AND TEAMWORK

Educator and reformer Roland Barth (2001) was bold enough to make the following claim, "I learned over and over again that the relationship among the adults in the schoolhouse has more impact on the quality and character of the school—and the accomplishment of youngsters—than any other factor" (p. 105). He couldn't be more correct. Effective organizations have a oneness, a community, that binds people together through thick and thin. They constantly stick up for one another and support each other. It takes time and effort to build relationships. It doesn't happen overnight. Organizations that go for quick transformation rather than build teamwork and relationships with sustained priorities over time are always disappointed and underachieving with the talent they have on hand. Paying attention to and fostering relationships is a benchmark of all high achieving organizations.

CHAPTER 6: FROM CONTROLLING MANAGERS TO SHARED LEADERSHIP

Leaders can win battles by using positional power with subordinates, and it may be faster to get results in the short run, but leaders cannot develop intrinsic motivation through positional power, and it takes intrinsic motivation to achieve breakthrough results. Relational power through shared leadership is the only way to achieve it. Shared leadership takes more time to develop, but once a worker becomes invested, their involvement in the vision of the organization increases. They become an asset to everything the organization is trying to accomplish. Long-range change and improvement is accomplished when leaders and workers become allies through shared leadership.

Leaders who deliberately and intentionally look for ways to share leadership wind up with empowered individuals around them willing to step up, learn new things, and take on new challenges. Leaders who insist on their own way will find themselves increasingly isolated, out of touch, and simply managing from one crisis to the next. As a matter of fact, if leaders are managing from crisis to crisis, chances are they are not moving in the realm of shared leadership.

CHAPTER 7: FROM HIDDEN AGENDAS TO AUTHENTIC LISTENING

Leaders who arrive with an agenda—or develop one without authentic listening—inhibit systemic change and improvement. Authentic listening involves actually putting yourself in the other person's shoes—to experience work and life as they are experiencing it to the greatest degree possible. It takes more than a little imagination to authentically listen. It also takes a heart to feel what the other person is feeling. Authentic listening frees us from having an agenda.

Blaming others is a hindrance to authentic listening. Authentic listening begins by removing all filters to data, and that can only be done through careful observation and soliciting the input of a variety of individuals. Change agents with agendas end up pushing *their plans* and the result will be a lack of buy-in and commitment from those around them. Authentic listening involves taking the time to feel the heart beat of the organization, and no two heartbeats are alike.

Authentic listening is more like sonar than a sounding board. It is listening with the intent to create movement. Sonar sends out a signal and waits for a response, so that the system can *act* upon that response. Authentic listening—like effective use of sonar—causes movement. It is a generator of change.

CHAPTER 8: FROM CONFORMANCE TO PERFORMANCE

Leaders who effectively initiate change that yields measurable improvement have to be willing at times to take a risk, step out of line, and see if anyone will follow. They are not afraid to generate tension in order to change the status quo. They understand intuitively that moving from conformance to performance will require the ability to effectively manage conflict and use tension as a generator for improvement.

There are many ways to introduce tension into a system. One of the most crucial, but often overlooked, is the necessity for tension in the executive team itself. A management team that does not use conflict as a tension generator will not arrive at the best ideas around the table. Every system requires tension—or adversity—to grow, change, and become stronger. Comfort, or equilibrium, is the enemy of growth.

Many leaders do not want to have conflict and avoid it like the plague. They don't want to make people uncomfortable. Unfortunately, the best ideas will not materialize without conflict. When teams are willing to face off and enter conflict, that is a sign of trust and commitment not only to other team members, but also to each one's willingness to commit to the team. Learning to engage in healthy conflict is not a one-time event, but an ongoing discipline that will lead to high levels of performance.

CHAPTER 9: FROM TRADITION TO DATA TO REFLECTION

Good decisions come from good data. There is simply no other way to look at it. The best companies know how to mine good data, and they use that data to make the best possible decisions, but they don't stop at just collecting data. They have learned how to reflect upon that data so that practice is changed. In education today, the data streams are endless, and we all nod our heads enthusiastically about the necessity to track data. However, organizations achieving breakthrough results don't just collect data, they *reflect* upon it and as a result make improvements.

A failure to make a conscious decision about what it is measured causes a lack of effectiveness and achievement. The most effective organizations base their decisions on fact, not popular opinion, and they are willing to go to great lengths to make sure they are getting the best information possible. Facing brutal facts and then having the courage and fortitude to do something about those facts is what puts school districts on the high road to systemic change.

CHAPTER 10: FROM ARRIVAL TO GROWTH

Effective change agents cultivate learning and discipline. They are disciplined about learning and always resist the feeling of arrival. New learning overcomes the feeling of arrival. Thinking you have nothing left to improve dooms an organization to not learning and growing. The leaders of tomorrow grew up with technology constantly improving every few years, and they understand there is always room for improvement and change is the vehicle for that improvement.

APPENDIX: PRIORITY LEADER ASSESSMENT

The book concludes with a self-assessment survey that readers can use to place themselves on each of the 10 priority leadership continuums. We believe this self-assessment tool will be extremely helpful to practitioners looking to apply the lessons presented and help others understand the concepts of the book.

Jim Collins, author of *Good to Great* (2001) discovered that the key to creating an environment of change is by not focusing on change. He argues that "under the right conditions, the problems of commitment, alignment, motivation, and change just melt away. They largely take care of themselves" (p. 176). Alignment with change comes first and foremost as a by-product of results and momentum—not the other way around. This book is about the conditions that create results and momentum.

This is not a how-to book because systemic change is too complex to be prescribed. Every setting around the country is different, and therefore, each vision created should be unique. This is a *how-to-be* book. Pursuing continuous improvement in each of the priority leadership continuums will generate measurable results. In a day and age when change becomes necessary for improvement, this book presents several new ideas and concepts for managing the untamed and often chaotic world of systemic change. We hope it will be embraced by the educational community and find a home in the world of business as well. Enjoy.

①

FROM PLANNING TO VISION

Creating visions should disrupt the status quo.

Gene Bottoms

One of the most important skills possessed by leaders is clarity of thought and speech about what they want to create. And because the clarity and the sense of empowerment leaders provide are contagious, individuals and organizations are transformed when these qualities are brought with persistence to various settings.

Dennis Sparks

"We have a plan! We are doing something! Look at what we've done!" Wrong. Many schools and districts spend so much time planning there is little energy left for implementation, and all of the time, energy, and resources spent building the plan could have been used discovering and implementing solutions. History and experience tell us most creative innovations happen when people deviate from the plan. It is innovation that breeds change—not extensive planning documents.

The mark of effective leadership is the ability to generate results. Genuine, measurable results and improvements come via change. Every effective leader that is bringing positive, meaningful systemic change to an organization has a vision. It is vision—creative passion—that drives change, not plans. Excessive and detailed plans can become a distraction from achieving meaningful results because so much time is spent building a great plan, we believe something has actually been accomplished.

Mike Schmoker's article "Tipping Point: From Feckless Reform to Substantive Instructional Improvement" (2004) thoroughly documents why planning has not resulted in any substantial school improvement and never will. You can't get there through planning. You get there through rigorous implementation of a vision driven by priorities.

When it comes to moving beyond planning, reformer Douglas Reeves (2004) boldly asserts, "In too many instances, strategic plans have become a singularity with the plan itself becoming the objective rather than the results the plan was to have achieved" (p. 60). He maintains that clear evidence of an over-emphasis on planning occurs when a task force disbands after "The Plan" has been developed. The message is all too clear to the workers in the field: the work stops once the plan is in place. Districts and schools committed to continuous improvement are driven by visions rather than plans.

It's been ten years since James Kouzes and Barry Posner discovered that "strategic planning does not work" (Kouzes and Posner 1995, p. 244). Mintzberg came to the same conclusion in his study, *The Rise and Fall of Strategic Planning* (1994), and Harvard Business School professor Gary Hamel told an audience, "You might as well dance naked round a campfire as go to one more semi-sacramental planning meeting" (Reeves 2002, p. 100).

There are only so many hours in a day. Every hour we spend compiling elaborate plans is one less hour we have to do the real work of improvement, which begins with vision. Defenders of the status quo tread water in the pool of procrastination, never able to achieve their destination, and the reason is simple. They do not have a destination because they do not have a vision. Just because the scenery keeps changing doesn't mean you are making progress. You could be just going in circles. Spending a lot of time making plans is the surest way to defend the status quo.

Planning is a job. Vision is a career. Planning is the task you force yourself to do, and most people need a steady diet of deadlines to keep motivated. Vision is a passion that comes from your soul—something you just can't help but doing. A vision keeps you up at night and gets you out of bed in the morning. Building plans is an extrinsic task that is usually required by some outside entity. Visioning is intrinsic. Nobody makes you do it. It is something that drives you to deeper and deeper levels of commitment and dedication.

Most plans are completed and put on a shelf somewhere. Consider the words of Helena Cronin, philosopher, social scientist, and co-director of the Centre for Philosophy of Natural and Social Science at the London School of Economics:

> The reality is that most documents of this nature (planning) reside in desk drawers and fail to impact what the organization actually does. Why? Environments change rapidly, and current priorities may not even be expressed in the documents. . . . Linear, mechanistic thinking, which still prevails in most organizations, is at odds with the emerging thinking about organizations as living systems. Unfortunately, many staff members are stuck in this old thinking. Thus, "That's not in my job description" is frequently heard when "Do whatever it takes to get it done" is the needed chorus in today's turbulent environment. (Rubin 1999, p. 330)

LEADERS HAVE A VISION

> If you want to build a ship, don't gather your people and ask them to provide wood, prepare tools, assign tasks. Call them together and raise in their minds the longing for the endless sea.
>
> Antoine de Saint-Exupéry

Martin Luther King was a man of superior vision. He was arrested and jailed on many occasions. He was stoned, stabbed, and physically attacked. His house was bombed. Day and night his phone would ring and someone would pour out a string of expletives. Frequently the calls ended with death threats. What kept him going in the light of such conflict? Certainly not his 5-year plan. It was his vision—his vision of a Promised Land where all races lived in harmony and mutual respect. That's what kept him going.

Gandhi was a man with a vision, and his compelling vision inspired his followers to create dramatic change. Gandhi was educated in the field of law in London, and when he returned to India in 1914, he was a very well-known and respected man. Within six years, he was elected president of the All India Home Rule League. The most remarkable thing about Gandhi's career was not his rise to power but his ability to communicate and to convince the people of India to use non-violent means for achieving their independence.

Gandhi had a strong vision—a compelling one. He believed and taught that nonviolence was the greatest force at the disposal of mankind. He believed it was "mightier than the mightiest weapon of destruction devised by the ingenuity of man." He asked the people to fight in non-violent ways, and eventually, they endorsed his vision with action. As a result of his vision, there was total commitment to his leadership. When he called for the people of India to burn foreign-made clothes and start wearing nothing but home-spun material, millions of people started doing it. Their struggle for independence was slow and painful, but eventually, in 1947, it was successful.

You will not find MLK's or Ghandi's 5- or 10-year plan. They didn't complete a process with that outcome in mind, but the world knows of their vision. It was their enduring, compelling vision that created meaningful change for millions of people. Not everyone can be a MLK or Ghandi, but we can each have a vision that will change the corner of the world where we live—provided that vision is the *right* one.

SOME LEADERS HAVE THE WRONG VISION

The collapse of Enron is a classic example of what can happen when leaders focus on the wrong vision. Harvard Business School professor Malcolm S. Salter has researched and written about Enron's demise (Salter 2003). The main story of Enron's collapse is a case of "ethical drift." In other words, at Enron, a team of executives created an extreme performance-oriented culture that institutionalized and tolerated deviant behavior. They were so concerned about the bottom line, they kept moving it to make themselves look better. Enron's vision was modeled after professional consulting firms, and most of these firms have a singular vision: "if there is cash to be made, then make it . . . nothing trades off against cash" (Webber 2002, p. 130). Enron was not able to keep their ethical standards and strategy when tempted by cash.

The company collapsed on December 2, 2001, and destroyed over $60 billion in market value. Their cave-in decimated thousands of people financially and produced a ripple effect that some markets felt for months. Near the end, 96 percent of Enron's reported net income and 105 percent of its reported funds flow were due to accounting violations. Enron's debt of $22 billion was underestimated by half (Lagace 2004). The Enron lesson illustrates that there is always a story behind the numbers. Priority leaders look beyond the numbers and develop their vision on what is right. They have a foundation beneath their success.

PRIORITY LEADERS HAVE THE *RIGHT* VISION

Maxwell (1998) states that leaders " . . . have a vision for their destination, they understand what it will take to get there, they know who they'll need on the team to be successful, and they recognize the obstacles long before they appear on the horizon" (p. 36). That doesn't mean they have a plan for avoiding those obstacles or even overcoming them. As a matter of fact, the most brilliant leaders decidedly do not have a plan, nor could they have conceived of one for overcoming the obstacles ahead. Instead, it is their vision, their driving ultimate purpose that keeps them going.

In Jim Collins' (2001) classic study of companies that made the leap from good to great results, he discovered that achieving greatness was not correlated to planning. As a matter of fact he was quick to point out "there is no evidence that the good-to-great companies spent more time on long-range strategic planning than the comparison companies" (p. 10). But he did find behind every great company there was a determined, strong-willed leader who held fast to a compelling vision—many times in light of circumstances and difficulties that were beyond impossible.

The world of sports is a microcosm of life, and there is much about priority leadership we can learn from its lessons. An all boys Catholic High School of 1,000 students in Concord, California, strung together one of the most remarkable achievements in sports—a football winning streak of 151 games, the most ever by any football team at any level. The De La Salle Spartans accomplished this without superior athletes or big budgets. Their remarkable achievement can be traced back to one man with a vision, Coach Ladouceur. "Everyone asks me how I've won 151 straight games," says Ladouceur. "My answer is always the same: 'By not concentrating on winning.' If you work hard enough, the wins will just come" (King 2004, p. 83). He never planned to win 151 games in a row. His vision was to create a great learning experience for his athletes. He was passionate about coaching, but not about football. He was passionate about instilling important life values to the student athletes in his charge.

When coach Ladouceur arrived at De La Salle 25 years ago, he found a handful of smallish boys with scant football knowledge who never had a winning season. Ladouceur immediately put in place an off-season conditioning program and taught his players a split back veer offense. Ladouceur hoped the simple system that depends on quickness and execution would help level the playing field against bigger and stronger opponents.

Within a year, the team went 6–3, and within 5 years they had an undefeated season. Recently they have strung together twelve straight Northern California championships and have beaten the toughest teams from southern California, Hawaii, and even the seven-time state champions from Louisiana. Although he has had job offers from several Division I programs, "Coach Lad" is still pursuing his vision at De La Salle. His remarkable success and achievement are a direct result of his vision and passion to coach his student athletes and help them become better people. His vision is not winning. His vision is preparation for life. Needless to say, he has the *right* vision.

Many sports enthusiasts claim John Wooden is the most successful coach of all time in any sport. In more than 40 years of coaching, he had only one losing season—his first. He led UCLA to four undefeated seasons and a record ten NCAA basketball championships. No other college team has ever come close. Wooden was driven by his priorities. His number one priority was not winning. His vision was getting his players to reach their potential. He was so driven by this singular vision that he never scouted opposing teams. His desire was not to win championships or even beat the other team. His vision was to help each team member to play to his potential and put the best possible team on the floor at all times (Maxwell 1998).

The success stories of Coach Lad at De La Salle and Coach Wooden at UCLA demonstrate that record-breaking results are not achieved by vision alone but by having the *right vision*. Paying attention to process: how people are treated, how ideas are generated and shared, and the discipline to do the right thing when no one is watching are all keys to insuring the proper process. In our results-oriented, win at-all-costs, competitive society, many leaders become clouded by the pressure to achieve rather than keeping their vision on the proper processes to generate those results.

The development of vision is something John Maxwell calls an *eagle environment*. "An eagle environment is one where the leader casts a vision, offers incentives, encourages creativity, allows risks, and provides accountability" (Maxwell 1998, p. 140). Public school systems are in dire need of leaders who can cast compelling visions and motivate others to join in the cause. Unfortunately, much to the detriment of school system improvement, most districts are still stuck in the quicksand of excessive planning.

PLANNING IN SCHOOLS

There is no end to planning in school systems. There are school improvement plans, district improvement plans, safety plans, technology plans, behavior support plans, teacher improvement plans, crisis plans, lesson plans, individual education plans, talented and gifted plans, 504 plans, and a host of other planning documents that consume the time, energy, and resources of those who work in schools. Some are federally mandated, required by the state, or another outside agency. At other times we impose the regulations on ourselves or create mythological barriers that do not exist.

As we get buried up to our eyeballs in the pile of plans, we must ask ourselves the most salient question of all: Do these plans bring about real change, or do they chiefly serve as defenders of the status quo and keep us from the real work of improvement and change in our school system? It is not that planning is inherently wrong. It is just that there are many, many things we could be spending our time on that are better, and in a world of resource reduction, the good becomes the enemy of the best.

SCHOOL AND DISTRICT IMPROVEMENT PLANS

Many states require districts to submit a district improvement plan, and most districts spend a great deal of time, energy, and resources developing that plan. Most districts further compound the resource drain by requiring individual schools to submit school improvement plans—everybody should suffer.

Upon completion, district improvement plans get sent to the state for "review." At the district level the hefty document could be hundreds of pages long. At the state department it's placed on the shelf among hundreds of similar plans. The state then sends back a piece of paper saying the plan was received. Whether or not that plan ever gets thoughtfully reviewed, studied, and looked at is anybody's guess, but our experience is that the plan *rarely* gets looked at by the state beyond the cursory acknowledgement it has arrived.

The reason is simple. It's not that the state department is lazy or doesn't care. They suffer from the same problem as those who work in schools. There is just too much to do, and not enough time to do it. The state *required* the document for the benefit of the districts with the hope that they learned from the process of building it, that the districts operate from it, and everyone is relatively happy—or as happy as one can be after developing these plans.

In moments of brutal honesty, nearly every principal and superintendent can tell where he or she put that district improvement plan and how often it is consulted. If the plan can be found a few months after it was completed, that is probably more than what half the school leaders can say. Many districts complete the plan in the district office laboratory far from children, turn it in, and it disappears from memory until the next time it has to be completed.

However, as educational reformer Douglas Reeves has discovered, more and more districts are learning how to shed hefty plans and make the transition to ones that are simple, focused, and useful.

Many school systems provide extraordinary examples of the principle of focus. The Norfolk Public School system in Virginia, for example, has only one board goal (Simpson 2003). This stands in stark contrast to school systems that appear to equate quality with girth in their school and district plans. The Freeport, Illinois, schools have made stunning advances in both educational achievement and in equity despite school and district plans that are remarkably brief. (Reeves 2004, p. 59).

SCHOOL IMPROVEMENT PLANNING IN LEBANON, OREGON

In Lebanon, we weren't happy with the amount of time spent building plans rather than developing vision, so we tried a different strategy with our recent state submissions. It was our intent to carefully define our priorities first and not be concerned about the length or complexity of the document. The result was an eight-page white paper describing the guiding principles behind our priorities without any emphasis on the strategic planning emphasis of goals, evaluation, actions steps, responsibility charts, and resource plans. It was mailed and took its place on the state department shelf among the hefty hundred page documents submitted by other districts. A few weeks later we received back from the state department the same one page acknowledgment letter that everyone else received. The one exception may have been our plan was actually read because of its brevity. We're not the only ones advocating for short, priority-based plans that are driven by vision.

Douglas Reeves has traveled the country and studied accountability systems for years. He's written several books on the subject. In his recent work, *Accountability for Learning* (2004), he cites examples of extraordinary improvement in Virginia, Illinois, and Indiana that all have one thing in common, "school and district plans that are remarkably brief" (p. 59). It's not the brevity that makes these districts excellent. It is their focus—their vision. Districts that have a laser-like focus on a few guiding principles have the best chance to see improvement and growth.

The fact of the matter is, no one really cares what your plans look like when you are successful. Plans only get scrutinized, reviewed, and second-guessed when you are losing. And herein lies the biggest irony of all. When you aren't getting the necessary results, people will demand to see your plans, and you will be forced to spend more time doing them. One weakness of the No Child Left Behind (NCLB) Act in its current form couldn't be more blatant. Low performing schools are required to improve because of their low performance. They are forced to create elaborate improvement plans. Creating these elaborate time intensive plans makes meaningful improvement that much more difficult to achieve.

Requiring any school system to develop elaborate planning documents only puts them at further disadvantage. When you have to spend a greater amount of time developing plans it means less time can be spent building vision, making changes, and trying new strategies. Unsuccessful organizations don't need to spend more time planning. They need to engage in more *innovation* and generate new ideas through inquiry and nimble strategy. Elaborate plans limit vision by creating boundaries that hinder innovation. Improvement comes via systemic change, and change is the result of innovation. Plans encumber improvement and systemic change.

In Lebanon, Oregon, we believe that the real work of improvement is not the building of the plan, but the implementation of priorities driven by vision. We have turned the tables on planning by forming school improvement teams facilitated by district leaders who meet monthly to constantly review data and design interventions based upon that data. We realize that student achievement is not just academic, but it is also related to behavior. Understanding this fact, we have designed and established teams based upon the continuous improvement model of Positive Behavior Support (PBS) developed by Golly and Sprague (2004) at the University of Oregon. We have added the academic component to their behavior model to create Positive and Effective Behavior and Learning Supports (PEBLS). Our PEBLS teams have a constant focus on academic and behavior improvement. They design interventions for small groups and individual students. They are trained to spend minimal time admiring the problem and maximum time developing and implementing solutions that will generate results.

BEHAVIOR SUPPORT PLANS

Let's take the classic example of planning gone awry that every principal knows intimately, behavior support plans. Behavior support plans and their first cousin, FBAs (functional behavior assessments), came into vogue with the 1998 reauthorization of the Individuals with Disabilities Educational Act (IDEA). When children are not behaving at school, the law requires a team of educators to conduct a functional behavior assessment to determine *why* the child is acting out. Nearly every principal and counselor has an FBA war story. FBAs can involve classroom observations, specialists, parents, educators (and lawyers) sitting around the table discussing and analyzing the question of: *why is this child acting out?*

After the FBA is drawn up, it is time to build the behavior support plan. Cadillac, lawyer-driven support plans can take hours and hours to develop. They are detailed documents sometimes written by outside consultants (who don't have to implement them) containing flow charts, diagrams, tables, and pages of text describing what to do and what not to do, depending on the child's behavior. They can be extremely complex documents.

Ninety-nine percent of the time they are not practical because children with behavior problems are not predictable, and no plan—no matter how elaborate—can cover every possible action of the child or every unusual circumstance they might face. The bottom line: elaborate, expert-driven support plans don't work any more often than simple ones, and schools that live by them end up stubbing their toes on them because the plans are too detailed and complicated to be followed exactly. When push comes to shove—and when lawyers are involved push always comes to shove—any lawyer worth the expensive suit will be able to pick apart some detail of the plan the staff didn't follow exactly, and you are in trouble.

NIMBLE PLANNING

When it comes to planning, our approach is to remain as nimble, flexible, and adaptable as possible. Nimble plans are effective and efficient because they are completed in a short amount of time by those who actually do the work. When it comes to students with challenging behavior, we write behavior support plans on a regular basis that can be completed in one meeting within 20 minutes. We are able to do this because we don't build plans for lawyers. We build plans for students. We focus on meeting the needs of the student, and when your focus is on a child's need, parents are supportive. Supportive parents don't call lawyers or run to the district office.

The real goal of any behavior support plan is to change behavior, not keep lawyers employed. Our support plans are effective because they are broad and focus on the vision of creating a positive individual who will benefit from schooling without interfering behavior. Nimble plans are easy to design, easy to implement, and simple to understand. They list desired behaviors, strategies to teach the desired behaviors, incentives for following them, and consequences when they are not followed. Because our plans are time efficient and effective, they can easily be written by teachers and counselors—even principals. As a result, we write them whenever we need to and they can be completed without outside help. They are easily revised when the strategies, incentives, or consequences need to be adjusted. Parents and students find them easier to understand because they are not full of educational jargon and flow charts.

Whether our focus is individual support for students with behavioral needs or wholesale school improvement, we must strive to fix our gaze on what is truly important if we want to develop visions that move our organizations toward continuous progress and breakthrough results. This can only happen when we determine to build the *right* vision for school systems.

BUILDING THE *RIGHT* VISION IN SCHOOL SYSTEMS

Leaders of high-performing schools have visions of what a school should do. They know how to support their visions with funding, time and other resources. They can retain their focus and carry most students, parents, and teachers, as well as the community along with them. These leaders know that developing leadership potential in others is essential to large-scale efforts and is a key to the primary goal of making sustaining gains in student achievement. Continuously examining visions and beliefs about the future sets the stage for motivating change and improvement. (Bottoms 2001, pp. 28–29)

What exactly is the right vision for school districts? Is there one right answer? Yes and no. The right vision for school districts is one that focuses on learning. The most effective kind of learning is engaging and emphasizes continuous improvement so that all students can be success-ful. Students should not be placed in learning environments where they are bored most of the time because they are further ahead than the ma-jority of other students. Likewise, students should not be placed in envi-ronments where they lack the skills to be successful. In other words, the right vision for school districts would be one that focuses on continuous improvement while simultaneously rejecting both social promotion and retention. Surveys of educators around the country generally agree with this assessment. The idea, or vision, of continuous progress is not up for debate as is the plan for achieving it, and that's why we resist planning.

There is no clear plan for restructuring public education to a continu-ous progress model, but that doesn't hinder us from trying to achieve the vision because we are not bound by the necessity of a plan. We can move forward without all of the answers. We can take steps without a clear plan in hand. Experimentation and innovation all occur before plans can be developed. Improvement begins with a vision and uses the lever of inno-vation to discover solutions that will eventually morph into a plan some-where down the line. In this model, the plan almost becomes an after-thought, a reflection of successful innovation that is true to the vision.

CONCLUSION: MOVING FROM PLANNING TO VISION

Vision generates results. Every effective leader that brings positive, meaningful change to an organization has a vision. Vision drives change, not plans. Planning is a threat to change because it is based on the sta-tus quo. Having an enduring vision will not generate a "to do" list, or a workable plan, but it will generate priorities that will ultimately guide change and lead to improvement.

We've been pursuing a vision of significantly increased student achievement in Lebanon, Oregon, for over seven years now. That vision has shown the way to three strong priorities: student achievement, sig-nature schools, and professional growth/accountability for staff. Work-ing these priorities has uncovered *targets of opportunity.* In pursuing these targets, we have seen improvement.

The trail we are traveling is not clearly marked, and it's been full of trial, difficulty, and obstacles. Sometimes the pace of change and pressure for

2

FROM GOALS TO PRIORITIES

Never doubt that a small, group of thoughtful, committed citizens
can change the world. Indeed, it is the only thing that ever has.

Margaret Mead

Effective leaders sustain momentum through difficult and trying situations by keeping the vision ever before the people. Visions are best artic-
ulated by priorities as opposed to goals. Priorities are long-range journeys
that call for commitment, and the only way to sustain them is through vision. Priorities are a state of being, the makings of journey. Goals are
short-term destinations. Goal setting is management. Pursuing priorities
is leadership. Systemic change does not come through goal setting. It is
birthed by a determined application of priorities that come from a vision
people can support.

At first glance, the difference between goal setting and priorities is
just semantics, but in reality the two concepts are fundamentally different. Understanding the difference is a major step in moving toward
a change agenda that will lead to improvement. Goals are short-term
destinations, achievable objectives. Priorities are the makings of a journey that require commitment. They are not achievable. They are the
pot of gold at the end of the rainbow. Management seeks to maintain

the status quo and is resistant to change. Leadership embraces change to generate improvement.

Priorities are states of being. Leaders without priorities lurch back and forth from one idea to another constantly in search of the quick-fix or the new secret to success. New superintendents come and go with each one trying to make a mark. And why do they want to make their mark? Because they just got hired and feel obligated to institute some kind of change, but many times the changes they pursue are not systemic because they are not anchored to the system's priorities. When the average superintendent does not last more than three years, it is almost impossible to introduce and sustain priorities, and priorities are the lifeblood of systemic change.

CHAORDIC: THE PURSUIT OF CHAOS AND ORDER

Dee Hock, founder of VISA and a mastermind of systems thinking and learning organizations, coined the term *chaordic* to describe the unique phenomenon behind successful organizations over the past 20 years. He noticed organizations that grow, change, adapt, and improve have a combination of chaos and order—hence the term "chaordic." He documents his findings and thoughts in his book, *Birth of the Chaordic Age* (1999). Hock asserts it takes more than chaos to cause an organization to improve, and by the same token, no organization gets better through order alone. There are always elements of self-organization, self-governing, and adaptive behavior in order to achieve breakthrough results.

In light of Hock's definitions, management represents order. Operations are controlled by schedules, due dates, and goals. Leadership reflects chaos—being willing to take risks and venture into the unknown in search of breakthrough results. It is through effective management that school district leaders can gain the trust of their staff, parents, and students. Effective managers return phone calls promptly; answer their e-mails regularly; follow up and follow through on discipline issues; make sure the schools are clean and safe; keep disruptions to a minimum; and perform a host of other activities that provide order and structure. Managers set goals and accomplish them. They have a "to do" list and work it every day. Effective management is more than enough to generate a guaranteed contract, but it is not enough to generate systemic change and breakthrough results.

Effective leadership challenges the status quo. It asks questions and often does so without the solutions in mind. Leadership looks for the answers to complex problems within the system through self-organization. Leadership does not impose its will. Leaders constantly seek to make the work become intrinsic because they know the best work comes from people that are committed beyond their paycheck. It comes from people who are passionate about what they do. Leaders develop and pursue priorities. They inspire others to do the same.

Effective administrators operate as both managers and leaders. They function as managers to build the confidence of the followers that is necessary for leadership to emerge. Good management is the foundation of an effective school, but leadership is the heart and soul, the bricks and mortar, where quality teaching and learning occurs. It is only through pursuing priorities that organizations can achieve long term, remarkable results that will last long after the original leader who instituted the change has left the scene.

Similar to planning in chapter 1, goals are not inspiring. No one is intrinsically motivated or inspired by plans and goals. They are boring. They are management. On the other hand, vision and priorities are inspiring. In this day and age, no one achieves breakthrough results without inspiration. Leaders who pursue remarkable results inspire greatness through priorities that are driven by a vision.

PRIORITIES IN THE MILITARY

General Norman Schwarzkopf (Maxwell 1998) knows the concept of priority driven leadership extremely well. Late in his career, he had the opportunity to command a brigade. He accepted a post others didn't want. The unit was the First Reconnaissance Commando Brigade of the Ninth Infantry at Fort Lewis, but it was called the "circus brigade" because of the lack of discipline and overall reputation as a group of misfits. Schwarzkopf instinctively knew that the soldiers in the brigade were capable. The real problem was that their priorities were wrong. He immediately rallied his officers and set new priorities. He had one vision is mind—get the troop ready for battle.

Armed with a vision and clear priorities, the unit began improving. It was only then that he set a goal: desert maneuvers the following summer. When the maneuvers came around the following summer, Swartzkopf's three battalions went up against thirteen marine battalions and defeated them soundly.

It's not that goals are bad, per se, it is only that goals do not drive wholesale, radical change. Goals are good as short-term events under the umbrella and direction of broad priorities. If Schwarzkopf had told his men that they were going to do desert maneuvers without first preparing them for the priority of battle, it would have been a miserable failure. Short-term goals will emerge once priorities are established and a direction is derived from them, but systemic change doesn't come from goals. It comes from priorities.

THE PRIORITIES OF GENERAL ELECTRIC

The legendary CEO Jack Welch of General Electric was one of the most successful business leaders of the modern era. When Welch assumed the leadership of GE in 1981, it was a good company with a 90-year history. The company stock traded at $4 per share and was worth about $12 billion, eleventh best on the stock market. This diverse company included 350 strategic businesses. He had a lot of reasons not to change anything. GE was a good company.

But Jack Welch believed the company could be better, and the only way to make it so would be through the rough waters of change. Within the first few months of taking office, he started something he called the hardware revolution. To each of the company's hundreds of businesses, he applied one simple priority: can the business be number one or number two at whatever they do in the world? Ten years later the result was remarkable. GE ended up with fourteen world-class businesses. All of them either number one or two in the world, and these businesses achieved greatness through the sales and divestment of all the rest of their businesses. The simple strategy paid off. GE's stock experienced a 2-to-1 split four times and is currently one of the most valuable companies in the world (Maxwell 1998). Welch was well known for his commitment to simplifying his organization around a few priorities. He believed every leader should be able to clearly explain the top three things the organization was working on, and if you couldn't then you weren't leading well (Byrne 2004). Jack Welch was a true priority leader.

SIGNS OF A PRIORITY LEADER

One of the key priorities for any company is to develop leaders that are intrinsically motivated to do the right thing when no one is looking. This type of leader is not driven by sweet compensation packages but by the desire to produce quality work and achieve success for the organization. They are leaders who are willing to give up personal success for the benefit of the organization. Many school superintendents don't last beyond three years, especially when they have to take on difficult decisions to keep the school district solvent.

Lebanon's superintendent, Dr. Jim Robinson, was faced with difficult financial decisions when Oregon's economy suffered a severe downturn in 2001. Rather than abandon the priorities of the district, he held fast to his commitment to the priority of student achievement. Over time, those decisions put Dr. Robinson on the wrong side of the teachers' union and resulted in a vote of no confidence. The most courageous leaders are willing to put their own careers on the line for the overall good of the organization. When it comes to school districts, students should come first.

Doing the right thing should become more important than maintaining the status quo in order to extend contracts. In the non-profit sector, taking on the status quo for the improvement of the organization is the number one way to shorten tenure. It happened to Dr. Robinson more than once. Critics say he never learned, but in reality, he never changed. He always put the overall needs of the students above his own sense for survival. Getting run out of town is the chance leaders take when you press on the educational reform level for too long and hard in one place. Over time, people get offended, and that offense can be your demise. In the for-profit sector, change agents who try improvements and generate results can exist as demanding taskmasters—as long as they achieve results.

THE POWER OF VOICE

Every effective leader has a voice, and they know how to use it. That voice, that passion, manifests itself in meetings, avocations for programs, and a variety of other settings. The voice can be heard and *felt* by others. It inspires change and disrupts the status quo. Their voice captures the vision and drives the priorities. It is the breath, the wind that fills the sails of systemic change and moves the organization forward.

All great leaders can be marked by their voice. Whether it was Martin Luther King's "I have a dream . . ." or JFK's "Ask not what your country can do for you . . . ," it is their voice that sets them apart. Leaders with voices don't have to say a lot, but they have something to say. When they talk, people listen, and more importantly, people act.

PRIORITY-BASED LEADERSHIP

Researcher Jim Collins (2001) discovered that every great company that surfaced in his research had what he termed, a "Hedgehog concept" (p. 95). According to Collins, the Hedgehog concept was a simple, abundantly clear priority that served as a basis for all their decisions. He also discovered this concept coincided with breakthrough results. "The good-to-great companies are more like hedgehogs—simple, dowdy creatures that know 'one big thing' and stick to it. The comparison companies are more like foxes—crafty, cunning creatures that know many things yet lack consistency" (Collins 2001, p. 119).

It is crucial for an organization to be able to boil down its one central mission to a few key priorities that will drive decisions into the future. In Lebanon, we identified three priorities: student achievement, signature schools, and professional growth and accountability (in the domain of teaching and learning). Student achievement in Lebanon is based upon a continuous progress model that defies traditional grade levels. It is a system that rejects both social promotion and retention.

Most classrooms in America are multi-grade classrooms. For example, most of the 10-year-olds are in fifth grade. Unfortunately, there is a wide skill range between the fifth graders. Some are second grade level in reading, and some are at seventh grade level. By contrast, in a multiage classroom students are grouped according to their level of learning. As a result, there is a much narrower band of skill, but a greater variety in ages, because children learn like they grow—in a widely diverse manner. Grouping by skill levels enables teachers to design a system of continuous progress for their students.

The means to increase student achievement is via signature schools. The priority of signature schools in Lebanon gives administrators the liberty to pursue innovations that will yield the greatest dividend in student achievement. School leaders in Lebanon are not encouraged to do everything the same way. Each principal is charged with the responsibility to seek out new and more efficient ways to accomplish the ultimate priority of student achievement.

The Student Achievement System (SAS) represents collective responsibility. Signature Schools represents corporate liberty. Both elements are essential to move a school system toward systemic change and breakthrough achievement. The SAS is responsible and accountable to produce children who can read, write, and think at ever increasing academic levels. The priority of signature schools provides the framework of liberty to pursue that responsibility in a way and manner that will ultimately result in success.

THE PRIORITY OF ACHIEVEMENT

When we introduced the Student Achievement System (SAS) in Lebanon schools we had a vision. We did not have a plan, nor make one, but we did have a vision. The vision was to do whatever necessary to improve the basic skills of students in reading, math, and writing. Because we were committed to the vision, we weren't afraid to challenge the status quo. The status quo in Lebanon was years of underachievement and social promotion.

We developed the SAS over a 7-year period of time to address the lack of achievement in our educational system. In rejecting social promotion and retention, we defined social promotion as moving students on to the next level of learning without the academic skills they needed to be successful, and retention as repeating a similar treatment to the one that failed the student the first time.

We surfaced this priority seven years ago and are still developing ever-greater levels of achievement in students. The true test of a priority is not whether arrival will happen because priorities are ongoing efforts of improvement. There is no arrival. However, there is a mark of success—ever-increasing achievement, and in Lebanon, we have seen historical achievement through our continuous progress model. Prior to the SAS, test scores in reading and math in Lebanon were far below state averages. We have seen our scores climb above the state average district-wide, and in some schools we have achieved the breakthrough result of 90 percent or more of students meeting and exceeding state benchmarks. All of our elementary and middle schools have far outpaced comparative schools.

The NCLB Act is body count legislation. The law calculates how many children failed to make standards and imposes sanctions on schools and districts that do not perform according to mandated goals. If NCLB is to truly honor its title, the law should not count failures but the time it takes for every child to achieve high standards. The SAS achieves the intent of NCLB because through it we can guarantee that truly, no child will be left behind.

When time becomes the variable, achievement can become the constant. In this way, we make sure that every child achieves. It may take some children longer, and they may need more accommodations, interventions, and support to make it, but that is exactly what the SAS enables us to do, and that is exactly what we can guarantee to our parents. Their child will not be left behind. Alternatively, the SAS affords us the luxury of letting some children progress faster through the achievement levels. Students who need less time can move forward without the boredom associated with waiting on others to learn before the group can go forward. Our model drives individualized, differentiated instruction, and it supports teachers to make that kind of teaching possible.

The SAS is a consultation model of educational progress. Parents and students are treated like clients rather than customers. Instead of parents and students wondering what grade the teacher "gave" and why, we have intelligent conversations around data that describe the level of learning a student has achieved, and what they need to advance to the next level of learning. Unlike a customer service model which dispenses grades and hard-to-understand reports, the client model informs, engages, and involves students and parents. Students and parents participate like they are going to the doctor for diagnosis and prescription rather than to a convenience store for a soda and potato chips. In our priority-driven, client-based model school has meaning. Progress is important and it matters. The result is systemic change and significant improvement.

THE PRIORITY OF INNOVATION

> Engagement in creative work energizes and increases teachers' and administrators' commitment to continuous improvement. Educators' capacity to invent solutions to educational problems is a powerful, untapped resource for improvement
>
> Sparks 2005, p. 16

We have come to realize that breakthrough results will be possible only with innovation, and to facilitate innovation, Dr. Robinson introduced the concept of *signature schools*. He realized early on that in order to achieve the adaptive challenges necessary to develop a continuous progress model, he would need to give each school the autonomy to act. Only through such autonomy would restructuring be possible.

Signature schools, by definition, are high achieving, invitational, and innovative. The expectation is achievement. The culture is invitational, and the means to achieve both is through innovation. In Lebanon, all schools are encouraged to innovate. The result has been a fertile ground for experimental calendars, afterschool programs, schools-within-a-school, and special schedules. Time has been reorganized through creative intersessions where portions of the student body return to school for intensive small group instruction. Some of the sessions focus on helping students who have not yet met standards and can greatly benefit from targeted, small group instruction. Other sessions focus on enrichment activities that expand the curriculum for students who have already achieved their benchmarks.

Lebanon High School received a substantial grant from the federal government to restructure into smaller learning communities and also received a grant from the Oregon Small School Initiative. After school programs have been developed where instructional aides trained in reading and math instruction lead groups of children in remedial efforts and split dismissal schedules where teachers work with small groups of children from their own classroom who have not yet met standards.

Signature schools are a significant departure from the traditional approach taken by most school districts that enforce high levels of standardization among their schools. Consequently, creativity is reduced, and a degree of sameness makes one school indistinguishable from another. Signature schools give building level administrators and faculty the liberty to create innovations that will lead to greater student achievement. Signature schools become a reality when principals and teachers own their innovations to the point they are willing to attach their signatures as endorsements of their creation.

THE PRIORITY OF QUALITY INSTRUCTION

Elmore and Burney (1999) make it clear that the most important element for school improvement is investment in instruction. They maintain, "it is about instruction and only instruction, and that instructional change is a long, multistage process" (p. 266). We agree. Realizing the importance of instruction, we developed a system of standards that define and support quality instruction. Our *Professional Growth and Accountability* (PGA) System, initiated in Lebanon in 2001, combines the notion of both intrinsic growth and extrinsic accountability to the profession of teaching.

The development of the third and final priority began in the fall of 1997 from the ground floor using the work of Charlotte Danielson (1996) as a framework. Over a three-year period, a team of administrators, teachers, and outside specialists developed a comprehensive system that describes what excellent instruction looks like, sounds like, and feels like. While it is true that defining quality teaching doesn't guarantee great instruction, the manual has given administrators and teachers alike targets to aim for in their quest for the continuous improvement of their craft.

A variety of instructionally embedded performance assessments and observations help teams of teachers constantly assess what students need to maximize their learning. Students who are not being successful are quickly identified and provided the resources they need. Our standards-based teacher framework for quality instruction provides both a floor of accountability for those who are extrinsically motivated, and a ceiling of growth for those who are intrinsically driven to greater and greater heights as a teacher.

During the last few years, we have put energy into designing standards for administrators that reflect the same high standards we have for teachers. The administrative professional growth and accountability system is framed around our three priorities of achievement, innovation, and quality instruction. Whereas the teacher system looks at individual classroom indicators, the administrative system considers school-wide indicators of excellence. The system sets forth high expectations and defines the targets for achieving those expectations.

THE PRIORITIES IN ACTION: PEBLS TEAMS

> A cardinal principle of measurement states that it is more effective and accurate to measure a few things frequently rather than many things once a year
>
> Reeves 2004, p. 59

In Lebanon we have developed teams that look at data on an on-going basis and make adjustments in order to improve. These teams carry out the work of our priorities. The Positive and Effective Behavior and Learning Supports (PEBLS) teams reflect on student assessment and behavior data and from that reflection design individual, small group, and whole class interventions according to student academic and behavioral needs.

We believe that behavior and academic instruction are the yin and yang of student achievement, and that managing student behavior is the first step to effective teaching and learning. Behavior begins with attendance and ends with safety, responsibility, and respect. When any of these elements are not present, the learning environment is compromised.

To increase levels of positive student behavior, Lebanon schools have implemented the research-based priority leadership concept known across the country as Positive Behavior Supports (PBS). This system was developed in conjunction with public schools by researchers at the University of Oregon, and outlined in their book, *BEST Behavior: Building*

Positive Behavior Support in Schools (Golly and Sprague 2004). The complex and effective system that has radically changed thousands of school environments for the better is built on three simple priorities: Be Safe, Be Respectful, and Be Responsible.

In the PBS system, school and classroom rules are taught in relation to the priorities of safety, respect, and responsibility. Incentives are given based on the priorities, and behavior plans are designed with those priorities in mind. As a result of this priority-driven system, the students quickly and completely learn the values of safety, respect, and responsibility, and they are able to internalize those values and apply them to their lives in the school environment and beyond.

Enough rules cannot be generated to cover every situation students face, and even if they could, students would not be able to respond to all of them. However, in a priority-driven behavior system, students are taught the basic principles, and then they are able to apply those principles in a variety of situations and circumstances.

Once student behavior is in place, there is only one missing element for high levels of teaching and learning to occur—quality instruction. Quality instruction is a function of academic support that is based upon student need. If a school has an effective core program in reading, writing, and mathematics, it will meet the needs of the majority of students (around 80 percent). They will be learning at high levels. However, in any school and classroom, there will always be students on either end of the continuum (high and low) that will need additional academic support and intervention to reach their potential.

These "fringe" students are commonly labeled TAG, ELL, or learning disabled. But regardless of their label, these students will underachieve if they do not receive the additional academic support necessary. Breakthrough schools develop interventions and supports to meet the wide range of academic needs that students possess. They have a singular focus on the priority of meeting student needs.

SYSTEMS THINKING: THE HEART OF PRIORITIES

Models of education that reflect continuous improvement are developed through systems thinking. It takes systems thinking to understand

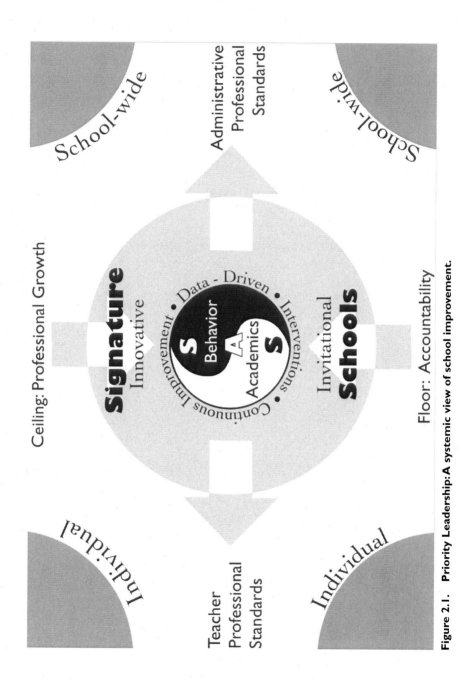

Figure 2.1. Priority Leadership: A systemic view of school improvement.

that everything we do is connected. When part of the system is struggling, it will affect other areas that are achieving. The whole is greater
than the sum of the parts, and the whole can only be achieved when
people work together in unison and mutual support. Education in
Lebanon is based upon the priorities of student achievement, innovation, and quality instruction, and we understand that these priorities are
connected. Each one affects the others. As a result, we have developed
the *Priority Leadership* graphic to illustrate how our priorities function
as a system; that is, a unified whole.

IDEAS: THE SOUL OF PRIORITIES

American author and social critic Midge Decter (1971) wrote the following:

> Ideas are powerful things, requiring not a studious contemplation but an
> action, even if it is only an inner action. Their acquisition obligates each
> man in some way to change his life, even if it is only his inner life. They
> demand to be stood for. They dictate where a man must concentrate his
> vision. They determine his moral and intellectual priorities. They provide
> him with allies and make him enemies. In short, ideas impose an interest
> in their ultimate fate which goes far beyond the realm of the merely rea-
> sonable. (p. 17)

In today's educational mainstream we strive to comply with new federal and state mandates. We honor policy and worship accountability.
Ideas and innovation are in short supply while conformity and compliance are the order of the day. Hope collapses when ideas are scarce.
When a system enjoys a free flowing supply of ideas life within the organization is made more vital and healthier. Ideas test our direction and
frame our priorities. They lead us to solutions and accomplishments.
Ideas create spontaneity, nimbleness, and creativity thereby allowing us
to adapt to the challenges we confront in our educational endeavors.

Creating a vision, setting our priorities, and feeding them with ideas
produces a change-oriented organization that is bound by its principles
and is on a firm course of action. This proactive approach fosters own-

ership and commitment whereas a reactive approach leaves ownership to the policymakers and develops conforming and complying behavior that fails to promote the overall health of the system. The value of ideas cannot be overstated. They are the soul of an organization.

CONCLUSION: MOVING FROM GOALS TO PRIORITIES

Mothers and fathers are often directing their children to "get your priorities straight." Workers are reminded to keep family high in their life's priorities. These are not admonitions for the moment but for a lifetime. As such, we are able to distinguish between goals and priorities. Priorities are for the long haul. They create a way of life. They are a state of being that defines us. Our ambitions and pursuits are represented by goals that are achievable and timely. They are transitory and re-established once met.

In today's public education systems, we lack a corporate sense of our priorities. We are dispersed in our thinking, and we seek to appease too many contrary demands. We don't know what we stand for or what is non-negotiable in our way of life. Still, we set our goals in pursuit of improved student outcomes. We quarrel over what those outcomes should be and how they should be measured. Why? It is simple. We've failed to establish priorities for our organizations.

3

FROM POLICY TO OPPORTUNITY

Don't let slip an opportunity; it may never come again.

Chinese proverb

It's too late to prepare when opportunity comes.

John Wooden

Stifled, fearful organizations are governed by policy. Leaner, result-oriented organizations are governed by principle, which allows them the liberty to pursue *targets of opportunity* when they arise. A system that is ruled by priorities or principles enables leaders to spend less time planning how to protect the status quo via policy and more time on innovations that present themselves as targets of opportunity.

Events that result in great achievement for companies and corporations are usually not the offspring of determined planning. More often than not, they are the result of a disciplined pursuit of the right opportunities that present themselves somewhere along the way. Being ready to pursue targets of opportunity opens up the door to innovation, and innovation is a generator of systemic change. Organizations on the lookout for targets of opportunity have a high tolerance for risk-taking and make their share of mistakes, but even more importantly, they unearth improvements and innovations that never would have been discovered otherwise.

School districts that achieve breakthrough results discover opportunities and pursue them relentlessly. A focus on problem-solving will keep a system operating smoothly, but identifying and capturing opportunities is the only way to make substantial improvement. Pursuing targets of opportunity is the trail to greatness. There is no paved road to greatness because few companies and schools ever get there. Great leaders don't necessarily know when the next opportunity will come, but they are willing to step off the road of mediocrity to pursue prominence, and as they travel, they are constantly on the lookout for opportunities. Many times they are able to locate them when other people cannot.

WHERE DOES POLICY COME FROM?

Policy generation is usually the result of a mistake or problem somewhere along the way that people want to avoid the next time around. The Enron collapse unleashed a host of corporate, policy-based reforms. The result has been more and more rules in a larger and larger code with smarter and smarter people trying to figure out how they can get around the new regulations (Salter 2003). We are not advocating for a policy-free environment. We understand that policy is important to establish guidelines and safety and to ensure proper working procedures, but we believe organizations that grow, change, and improve are not *governed* by policy to the point where they miss targets of opportunity.

The management of school districts relies on policy manuals, handbooks, and other rule-based documents. The more emphasis that leaders give to these documents of conformity the less likely a reform agenda is operating in the system. While every system needs standard protocols for doing business, the extent of their use should be to the least degree possible while still operating in an orderly environment. The overreliance on rules suppresses the capacity of the system to be nimble and in a state of readiness to seize opportunities to improve the system.

Rules create compliance behavior while opportunities create innovation. Rules are necessary for order, but they should not seek to drive or control the organization. The reason is simple. Organizations are systems, and systems cannot be controlled. Systems can only be *disturbed* (Pascale, Millemann, and Gioja 2000). Schools and districts should be influenced by innovation where the rules are made to work for the changes that are necessary to improve the outcomes for all. When a new situation arises, leaders often ask, "What's our policy on that?" The better question is, "What opportunity does this situation create for us?"

WE'VE NEVER DONE IT THAT WAY BEFORE

Governance by policy hinders innovation by constantly reinforcing the most dangerous and preventive change statement of all: "We've never done it that way before." When it comes to developing an improvement oriented culture, that statement in itself should be the number one reason why you do something different.

In 1998, Intel's head of the logic-technology Youssef El-Mansy told an elite team of scientists that he would like them to publish a paper stating they had designed the fastest transistor in the world. He didn't tell them how to build it. He only established the outcome. In doing so, he made it necessary for the scientists to rethink their basic approach to design. The team soon realized they couldn't use silicon dioxide, the insulator that Intel had been using for more than three decades because the push to make everything smaller had effectively made the insulator obsolete. There was too much of a heat loss. Divorcing silicon dioxide freed the scientists to pursue targets of opportunity with other materials. The result was the TeraHerz chip—cooler, faster, smaller, and smarter. It has paved the way for the next generation of computer processing innovation (Anders 2002).

Another strategy Intel uses to inspire innovation is to take their newest hires, generally new Ph.Ds, and assign them to the toughest projects. The new hires are not governed by policy. They don't know the rules yet. No one has told them what is impossible or which problems are unsolvable. Such a strategy often results in new breakthroughs.

MOVING FROM POLICY: FLEXIBLE JOB DESCRIPTIONS

At Southwest Airlines anyone on the ground staff can do any function, even the supervisors. Some union contracts don't allow that—they have "covered work." There is no covered work at Southwest. The job descriptions all say at the end, "and whatever you need to do to enhance the overall operation" (Gittell 2003, p. 155).

Having flexible job descriptions is one way to point an organization toward targets of opportunity and away from a policy-driven environment. Traditional job descriptions assume that the same tasks and skills that are relevant at one point in time will continue to be relevant in the future. They focus on specific tasks rather than the broader behaviors that are needed to achieve success—like teamwork, confidence, and trust. Static job descriptions do not factor in the importance of on-going change that is necessary for improvement to occur.

Increased flexibility in job descriptions leads to higher labor productivity because the flexible job boundaries help to build stronger relationships among employees. They learn to help each other in times of need. The result is increased communication, coordination, trust, and morale among the various employee groups (Gittell 2003). When job descriptions are flexible, it enables workers to place the priority on getting the job done rather than simply following policy dictates.

TARGETS OF OPPORTUNITY IN THE MILITARY

Over the last 50 years, the United States military has been accustomed to developing strategic battle plans and following the rules of engagement when entering a conflict. With the emergence of terrorist forces, the military has become more nimble by developing a state of readiness where they can move swiftly to strike targets of opportunity. The war on terror has generated an entirely new approach to warfare.

There are lessons for district administrators in this approach. If school leadership develops a keen state of readiness for improvement then directors can take advantage of the opportunities as they present themselves. This is nothing new. Any school district that has created a new school, program, or innovative project knows this to be true. Somewhere in the development stage, an opportunity is presented that the developers could not have seen. It was beyond the plan. Those that are willing to seize those opportunities push open the door to innovation and systemic change. If we are driven by strategic plans and policy manuals opportunities will frequently pass us by because we are too busy maintaining conformance to the status quo.

OPPORTUNITY IN ATHLETICS

Athletic contests and the officials that govern them present another example of the transition from policy to opportunity. Referees must have a thoroughly developed and exhaustive knowledge of the rulebook and the interpretations manuals that accompany it. However, once the game begins there is no time to refer to the document or even to recite the principles for fair play. Referees are taught to honor the rule book by calling the contest "within the spirit of the game" not "by the book." These two ways of governing must be congruent, but the former is preferred to the latter because it lets the official apply knowledge to the situation at hand. The context of the situation is anticipated in the official's decision making.

As school district officials we must make our calls within the spirit of the game. Our game is the improvement of the system for the increased learning of our students. When we are operating in that context we must remember what is in the rulebook but make our decisions based upon our best application of that knowledge to every given situation. There is a certain freedom from rules that comes with this approach. The reward is the increased capacity to make decisions that take advantage of situations as they emerge.

NCLB BODY COUNT

The NCLB is a federal accountability measure designed to gauge institutional effectiveness by determining a percentage of students who succeed on various achievement measures. This "body count" determines whether we are winning the war on illiteracy. NCLB is a policy driven agenda that accomplishes the opposite of its own intent. Schools and districts "hunker down" and attempt to comply by working harder and doing the same things better. If we were really intending to improve the performance of school systems, we would find ways to inspire district leaders to re-create instructional delivery where time would no longer be the constant and achievement the variable. School districts would build the reciprocal structures and declare time as the variable and achievement the constant. If that were really the case, then no child would be left behind because "being behind" is time sensitive not achievement sensitive.

To undertake such an innovation would mean reinventing schools so that social promotion and retention are minimized. Our current factory conveyor belt system of public education forces one or the other. When annual grade levels are used to organize the system, we arrive at year's end and need to make a decision for those students who are not "keeping up." We must choose to socially promote or retain them. When this occurs, each child becomes a part of the body count. However, to change the current structure would be terribly risky in the face of mandated yearly testing and federal accountability. We elect to play by the rules to keep necessary funding to the disadvantage of children. The spirit of NCLB is worthy. If only we could play by the spirit of the law rather than its letter.

AN OPPORTUNITY SEIZED: THE STUDENT ACHIEVEMENT SYSTEM IS BORN IN LEBANON, OREGON

When Dr. Robinson assumed the helm of Lebanon schools in the summer of 1998, he soon realized that the school system suffered from an inferiority complex. Lebanon was always below average in student achievement. Community forums quickly surfaced the key issue. Students were progressing from grade to grade without the necessary academic skills to be successful. The end result was a high school full of students ill-prepared to achieve. They were on trajectories of failure that even the most elaborate high school recovery and alternative programs couldn't fix. Like many places across America, Lebanon was really good at social promotion, and they ought to have been. They'd been practicing it for a long time.

In spite of over two decades of daunting retention research that concludes students who are held back become prime targets for future failure, Dr. Robinson seized an opportunity to make a difference. With encouragement from the school board, district leadership created the Student Achievement System (SAS), a systematic way of measuring student achievement that created yearly performance targets for students based on state tests and district performance assessments. Promotion standards were developed in reading, writing, math, and speaking. Students had to demonstrate mastery on state tests and district performance assessments before they would be promoted to the next grade level. For the first time, students had to demonstrate what they knew and were able to do. With one big push, the pendulum was sent swinging away from social promotion and toward retention. As you can imagine, the system was sent into an immediate disequilibrium.

Initially, teachers, students, and parents were in an uproar. Principals soon found out that talking about achievement and taking drastic steps to implement achievement were two very different things. Increasing student achievement was a great idea that looked nice on paper, but taking a bold step to impact it through promotion standards was painful. That first year, 15 to 20 percent of the students were unable to meet the standards and were afforded more time at their current grade level, and though some parents struggled with the new standards, teachers had difficulty with retention as well. It was crushing for them to share the bad news with parents that their child would be repeating a grade level.

Some parents, however, had a different response. They were pleased that the district was taking a bold step toward guaranteeing achievement, and though retention was never preferred for a child, it was appreciated because many parents instinctively realized that moving their child forward without the necessary academic skills would only ensure future failure at some point.

However, over time, the unintended consequences of the retention program began to surface. Students who were retained were losing motivation and feeling defeated. They missed the mark for promotion and were now sent around the carousel again. Holding students back a year was in many cases a demotivator, and the only thing worse for a teacher than an under-skilled student is an *unmotivated*, under-skilled student. Through hard work, effective instruction, and a great deal of effort, students with low skills can achieve over time, but the unmotivated and under-skilled just get further and further behind. That experience, coupled with the body of research regarding retention, convinced administrators that retention was not the solution either.

It was during this time that the SAS moved to the next level. Rejecting social promotion and avoiding retention requires a restructuring of the educational system around the resource of time, and this can only happen when a new paradigm is conceived regarding equity. True equity relentlessly seeks to meet the needs of each individual student.

It became clear that we would not be able to meet student needs without taking on the adaptive challenge of finding the balance between social promotion and retention. In its current form, the SAS rejects both social promotion and retention, with social promotion defined as sending students on to the next grade level unprepared academically, and retention defined as doing the same thing for two years in a row. What has emerged in the Lebanon schools can now be seen as the beginning stages of a continuous progress model.

In Lebanon schools, students advance to the next level of learning when they are ready. The result has been remarkable. Grouping the schools by benchmarks rather than grades has created natural teams of teachers who work with groups of students with similar abilities. Students move through the benchmarks according to their learning and performance. Some students are able to move considerably faster, while others get the benefit of more time. The question has shifted from "Did they meet the standard?" to "What are we going to do differently so that they can meet the standard whenever they are ready?" We've also stumbled upon a new paradigm that occurs even more frequently, "Now that they've met the standard ahead of schedule, what are we going to do so that their learning is not slowed down?"

Learning, like the development of the human body, is not static. Not everyone makes a year's growth in a year's time—and that shouldn't be the expectation. Some students can make two years or a year and a half of progress in a year, and some students might only make a half-year's growth. In our ungraded schools, students move seamlessly from one level to the next all in cooperation and communication with parents. We have shifted our spotlight from impartial standards to student need, and since student need is the focus, there are no limits to what students can achieve. The result of pursuing the purest form of equity—meeting each student's need—has been liberating. In this way, every student is not only motivated but successful as well.

The SAS did not begin as policy. It began as a target of opportunity and only became policy once it was found to be successful. And that is a key difference for priority leaders. Priority leaders hunt for opportunities and pursue innovations. It is only after they are found to be successful that the innovation becomes policy. In this way, only what is proven and important enters into the policy books. Traditionally, leaders and boards use policy to create change. Untested policy designed for a particular outcome is implemented in the hope that it will coerce workers into following a certain set of guidelines or rules to accomplish a particular goal. Priority leaders view this technique as backward. They do not use policy to implement change. Instead, they discover what works by pursuing opportunities, and once they are proven to be successful, policy is developed which has a way of "sealing the deal," and making the innovation a part of the system. Creating policy when innovations become successful protects organizations from the bane of policy—unintended consequences.

UNINTENDED CONSEQUENCES— A CASE STUDY OF IDEA

Steven Gillon (2000) wrote a book entitled *That's Not What We Meant To Do*. The book documents reform in twentieth century America and the unintended consequences of well-intentioned policy. History is full of such examples, and educators don't have to look much farther than 1975 to find a stellar example. Policymakers had great intentions when the Individuals with Disabilities Education Act (IDEA) was created in 1975. Educators were going to find those disabled kids. The ones we were not serving. The ones society had rejected, and they were going to help them. Sometimes people think before 1975, students with disabilities were not receiving services. Not true. At the time of the law, 8 percent of the student population was receiving special education services. However, a federal research study declared that in reality, over 12 percent of the population was actually disabled. The policy that passed in 1975 was a direct result of the study, and "child find" became law. School districts had to find the students who were not being served. Educators and consultants converted Winnebagos into testing centers to find those disabled kids—the quota of 12.1636 percent must be met or funding would be lost (Edgar 2005).

The unintended consequence of this policy driven initiative was disastrous. Not only did the 1975 law create hoards of unnecessary paperwork, but educators became so desperate to find disabled kids that students who were not disabled were being identified and labeled as such. English Language Learners (ELL) and others were determined disabled simply because they hadn't learned English yet. Funding was removed from schools if they didn't hit their quota of 12 percent. When the specialists couldn't find disabled kids in parking lot malls, they turned back to the schools and asked teachers about the struggling students in their classrooms, maybe they were disabled. As a result, students who were absent too much or moved around were labeled disabled and given services. Even victims of poor instruction were sometimes labeled! The unintended consequence was a *reduction* of services for those students who had true learning disabilities, and an increase of paperwork for the very teacher who had to deliver the services. There were good intentions behind IDEA in 1975, but the policy resulted in increased paperwork for learning specialists, more students to serve (many of whom were not disabled), and a reduction in services for the truly disabled. Policy-driven reform often has unintended consequences, and we are still reeling from IDEA and its subsequent revisions.

Students who are struggling to learn need intensive interventions early before the learning gap becomes insurmountable. The current identification system requires students to demonstrate a gap between their ability and performance before they can receive services, and many times that gap does not surface until the child is in third or fourth grade. Everyone knows it's too late by then to make much of difference without vast resources. What could have been corrected with a year of effective small group instruction in first grade becomes a 3- or 4-year problem by the fourth grade, and the sad part is a skilled first grade teacher or special educator can easily identify the difficulty in first grade, but policy prevents them from helping. The truly disabled will need help throughout their school career, but it's the slow learners we are hurting with the policy structure of IDEA. Fortunately, the most current revision of IDEA allows districts to identify needy students in ways other than the gap or discrepancy model so that services can be provided earlier, but 30 years of tradition will not unravel quickly, and it may take years before the reform significantly changes how schools operate.

Providing students specialized instruction by reading experts before they qualify for special education is a target of opportunity that defies policy. Schools that meet student needs pursue those kinds of opportunities whenever they can. At Pioneer School in Lebanon, Oregon, we a have a team structure that identifies every needy student classroom by classroom that absolutely guarantees no child will be left behind. Children get the interventions they need, from resource rooms or Title I, before they become disabled. It is the sensible thing to do, and it is one of the chief reasons a K-8 school such as Pioneer with a free and reduced lunch count of 70 percent has achieved over 90 percent of their 500 students meeting and exceeding state benchmarks. The story of Pioneer's achievement is recorded in the book *Excellence, Equity, and Efficiency* (Hess 2005).

WHERE WILL NCLB TAKE US?

Thirty years ago IDEA started with good intentions and resulted in poor outcomes. NCLB began with good intentions—that's why the law passed. It had strong bipartisan support. Senator Hillary Clinton wrote many of the most important amendments to the law. When the bill was signed, a congressional delegation including Senator Edward Kennedy and President George W. Bush toured the country to praise its contents (Reeves 2004).

Educators believe in success, and we want all children to achieve it. However, we are beginning to see unintended consequences as a direct result of NCLB's passage. There are stories around the country of schools that in their focus to stay off of Adequate Yearly Progress (AYP) lists have put too much of an emphasis on raising test scores via low level thinking (drill and kill activities) and cut programs that do not directly support math or reading (Littky 2005). We do not necessarily need more policy to achieve accountability. As more and more public schools are labeled as failures, and as schools are reconstituted as a result of NCLB's punishment-based model, it makes one wonder what kind of unintended consequences we will be looking at three, five, or ten years down the road as a result of this legislation.

The bottom line is clear. Priority leaders understand that punishment-based policies are not the way to create innovation, change, improvement, and accountability. Punishment-based systems create environments of fear and mistrust, and no one does their best work in a fear-based environment.

Dr. W. Edwards Deming, the father of the concept of total quality management (TQM) and continuous quality improvement was adamant that leaders need to remove all fear-based barriers if they are going to create environments where people achieve quality outcomes (Deming 1986). Quality does not happen without people doing their best work through continuous improvement and innovation. Environments known for opportunity rather than policy till the ground for innovation and the discovery of best practices. Organizations run by priority leaders form their own standards of accountability that make more sense and are higher than anything outsiders can impose.

THE POLICY OF "RESEARCH-BASED BEST PRACTICES"

There are times when the good becomes the enemy of the great. Educators believe in best practices. The talented ones are constantly looking for ways to improve their practice. They get ideas from wherever they can, but they do not have a love affair with the university league's "best practice" rhetoric. The reason is simple—best practice doesn't always mean most effective. The problem with proponents of best practice is something that is effective as an innovation in one location becomes policy in the next, and as soon as it becomes policy, the practice becomes less effective. There are no practices so much better than the rest that they achieve teacher proof status. No "best practice" is so superior it will grow wherever you plant it. *Teacher quality* is still the most important single influence on student achievement (Marzano 2003; Reeves 2004; Sanders 1998).

Author Todd Whitaker, in *What Great Teachers Do Differently* (2004), speculates that the "open classroom" innovation of the 1970s got its start when a couple of truly talented teachers had to teach in the gym because of overcrowded classrooms. They worked together and transformed the gym into a first class learning space for their students. Other educators heard of the fantastic learning that was happening and sent teams over to see it. Studies were conducted. Results were proven. Books were written. Best practice was established. Before long, classrooms without walls began springing up all over the country. It was also during this time that researchers told us having windows in classrooms would be a distraction to students' learning. Districts passed policy and built windowless buildings with open classrooms in mind. In 1975 it was a great idea. Ten to fifteen years later the walls went up and windows went in. Educators discovered that open classrooms and team teaching wasn't for everybody, but it still works for somebody. And somewhere in America there is still some great teaching and learning going on in an open classroom. It's just not best practice anymore.

Priority leaders do not look for one solution and then create policy that makes everyone do it. Teaching is not rocket science. It is more difficult. Every district, school, and classroom is its own mission to Mars. In rocket science there is a prescribed pattern. Get the materials, follow the pattern, build a rocket. Teaching is more complex because we are working with humans, and people don't come with instruction manuals. In the world of teaching and learning, there are a variety of complex and often confusing messages about what can and can't be done and reasons why things work and why they don't work. Every *person* is different. There are nuances in every setting that make significant differences in how programs may or may not work. Every setting needs its own solution based upon the demographics of the community, district, school, and even classroom. There are principles that carry over, but the process to achieve those outcomes will be different.

Priority leaders understand there are targets of opportunity, chances upon which to capitalize. Effective systems and programs elsewhere must always be adapted to the new setting. Policy is not enough. Priority leaders resist policy. Rather, they look for opportunities to act.

CONCLUSION: MOVING FROM POLICY TO TARGETS OF OPPORTUNITY

Carnivores are skilled hunters who use every available sense to seek out their next meal. They enjoy keen eyesight. These creatures have deft hearing and are fleet of foot. They are constantly surveying their surroundings in search of opportunities. When they have identified the opportunity at hand they become intensely focused and action-oriented. Educational reformers stress that effective leaders take action and don't wait for everything to fall into place. They understand that learning happens along the way, and they are not afraid to get started (DuFour 2003; Lindstrom and Speck 2004). Such is the behavior we should employ when leading school districts. We should not be focused on the operational elements or the laws, policies, and mandates of the educational system, but rather constantly surveying our environment for opportunities to better the system. When an opportunity is recognized we should be organizationally nimble enough to attack it with vigor. If we are constrained by rules then these opportunities will walk right on by.

4

FROM PROBLEM-SOLVING
TO CAPACITY-BUILDING

Lead yourself, lead your superiors, lead your peers, employ good
people, and free them to do the same. All else is trivia.

Dee Hock, Founder of VISA

Leaders become leaders because they want to help people, and many
times they help people by solving their problems—being the hero. Unfortunately, stepping in to solve problems does not build capacity in followers. It enables the status quo. Staffs do not learn new ways of thinking and working when leaders constantly intervene. The art of
delegation, the ability to build capacity, is a learned skill that does not
come easily to leaders who like to step in and save the day. Delegating
leadership roles to others and then stepping back and giving them authority to act is the most effective way to build capacity. It's simply a
matter of doing the math. Ten people enabled to do their best will accomplish much more than one superstar.

Steven Sample, president of the University of Southern California,
led its successful turnaround and wrote a book entitled, *The Contrarian's Guide to Leadership* (2002). Sample takes delegation one-step further. He argues that great leaders *work for* those who work for them. In
other words, once the right people are hired, the priority leader does

whatever necessary to make those under him or her successful. It's not just a matter of viewing subordinates as equals, but actually working for them by listening to their ideas, helping them formulate vision, and doing whatever possible to help those visions become reality.

INTRINSIC MOTIVATION: A SIGN OF HIGH CAPACITY

The more staff members become reliant on themselves and each other to solve problems, the more intrinsic and disciplined a team becomes. Almost all effective innovations that create change stem from workers increasing capacity through intrinsic motivation and spreading that innovation to others. Intrinsic motivation comes from the heart—where passion lies—and is not overcome by outward pressure. Intrinsic motivation is the driving force behind champion athletes, great inventors, and successful business people. In the same vein, it takes intrinsic motivation to achieve breakthrough results in school improvement.

In many circumstances motivation begins extrinsically before it becomes intrinsic. The connection between capacity-building and intrinsic motivation cannot be overstated, and neither can the fact that motivation usually begins extrinsically. Whether it is a weight loss program or a workout schedule, the power of peer pressure and accountability are tremendous initial, extrinsic motivators. Over time motivation has the opportunity to move inward and become a lifestyle change.

In schools, we are trying to create "lifelong learners." That is a high calling—so high we would venture to guess many administrators and teachers are not operating in that category themselves. One doesn't become a life-long learner until one *chooses* to invest time and resources in the process. Ask a group of administrators how many books they've read about leadership or education in the last year, journal articles they've read, or better yet, articles they've written. The results may surprise and even terrify you.

Ask a group of teachers the same question. Are they taking that class on reading instruction because they love the subject and want to help their children read better or do they have to get their credential renewed? Most of the learning related to work that is happening all around us—in every field—is extrinsically motivated in some way. And that is OK to start with, but breakthrough results will only occur when that motivation goes inward. When motivation goes inward, it replaces fear, lack of confidence, and other barriers to learning and achievement.

Leaders who spend their time solving the problems of those around them create dependent followers. The goal is to create intrinsically motivated leaders who take on challenges and risks because they seek improvement. In this way being understaffed and overworked is a blessing in disguise because people have to take on new jobs and share jobs they wouldn't normally tackle. They also learn to stop doing things that don't make a difference because there is no longer time or resources to do them. Stepping out of your comfort zone in that way builds capacity for improvement.

PROBLEM-SOLVING CONSUMES TIME

Administrators often complain there is inadequate time to accomplish all of the work set before them. At the same time they can be found moving from one problem to another throughout their day. Staff appreciates this trail of problem-solving in the school. It is valued even to the extent that problem-solving is high on the virtues list when selecting new administrators. Hiring committees can often be heard to ask for a "real problem solver." The presumption is that problem-solving is a leadership skill of the highest order.

In fact, problem-solving by its very nature is a reaction to a situation or circumstance that must necessarily be pre-existing or emerging. The problem leads and the leader solves. Add to that the assumption it is the leader's job to problem-solve and you create the conditions for a management/leadership imbalance that will stall movement toward the school's vision. Fixing isn't building. To avoid fixing situations it is necessary to develop that capacity in others who are more suited to the resolution of the issues at hand.

If the leader engages in problem-solving singularly and others become overly reliant upon the leader to do so, the environment will be one of learned helplessness and passivity in the followers and frustration in the leader. A successful administrator builds capacity for problem-solving in all of the affected people within the school. This is more the leader's task, which is to enable the followers to solve their own problems while moving the school toward its vision.

It is important to view with skepticism the acclaim of the followers that a leader is a great problem solver. It is surely important to have problem-solving skills, but it is quite another matter to employ them when others are equally capable. Simply put, a problem solver looks for solutions while a capacity builder looks for ideas. In a high capacity school, problems seem to "fix themselves" because everyone is willing to step in and do what is necessary to solve issues that arise. There is no line of people outside of the principal's office waiting to have their problems solved. Time is created for principals to lead via innovation.

If the leader deflects the problem to those who are nearest to the issue at hand and who have the capacity for its resolution, then time is preserved for the leader to address the root causes behind the problem rather than the existing conditions of it. Problem solvers react to existing conditions but do not seek to change the conditions that created the problem in the first place. Capacity builders have a vision for what can be and constantly change the conditions so that a new, improved future and way of being can emerge. In order to build capacity in followers, the leader may even create more problems!

BUILDING CAPACITY CREATES TIME FOR INNOVATION

When Dr. Robinson first came to Lebanon, he received dozens of phone calls every week from upset and dissatisfied customers because "things weren't right down at that school." He was amazed by the rate and demand for problems to be solved. Over the last seven years capacity has increased throughout the schools, and there is a whole lot less problem-solving that goes on down at the superintendent's office.

Capacity for problem-solving was developed in each school through the concept of *Signature Schools.* Through training, Dr. Robinson encouraged each school to develop a signature, something they would be known for and own, that would set them apart from the rest of the schools in the district. The notion of signature schools began as a quest for uniqueness and over time developed into displays of innovation and ownership.

Schools throughout the district experimented with a variety of after-school programs, split dismissals, technologies, advisories, team structures, scheduling options, inter-session calendars, bus schedules, interventions, creative small grouping techniques, and new instructional methods all in an effort to discover innovations to develop their signature. The by-product of these innovations was an increased capacity in every school. Schools now had the responsibility to find their own solutions to the problems they discovered within their system, and the priority of signature schools afforded them the liberty to make the necessary changes.

BUILDING CAPACITY TO SOLVE BEHAVIOR PROBLEMS IN SCHOOLS

One of the biggest and most frustrating time drains for principals is dealing with recurring student misbehavior again and again. There is no greater way to burn out a principal than constant doses of behavior referrals. When capacity is built for teachers and staff to handle their own student behavior problems, time is created for the principal to focus on leadership issues instead of management ones. There are many effective schoolwide behavior programs on the market. The Lebanon School District has chosen to invest its time and energy in Positive Behavior Support (Golly and Sprague 2004) that focuses on training the *adults* in the building how to respond to student behavior so that student behavior is changed. The focus of PBS is preventive and instructional rather than punitive.

When every adult in each building is speaking the same language and teaching the same rules and expectations, there is tremendous power to not only change the behavior of students but to fundamentally change the culture as well. The result of such positive change and culture transformation is a capacity builder that will yield dividends in student learning.

Creating schools with a high capacity for handling their own behavior problems begins by establishing boundaries—expectations that govern behavior. In an expectation-governed system, every rule is stated positively as an expectation, not negatively as a punishment. As a result, students are taught appropriate behaviors and those behaviors are reinforced through a system of positive rewards and logical consequences. This system is not just a good idea. It has a strong research-based track record and a history of demonstrated success in a variety of settings and schools around the country.

Schools that implement PBS generally notice a 50 percent reduction of office referrals within the first year. Those are the kinds of results worn-out administrators dream about, and the extra time and energy administrators gain through effective PBS implementation can be directed toward the instructional leadership of the building rather than being the disgruntled warden. PBS is one example of how schools can increase their capacity for problem-solving behavior. Helping struggling students is another area with lots of room for capacity-building.

BUILDING CAPACITY TO SOLVE ACADEMIC PROBLEMS

Schools across the country are turning to the power of teacher teams to build capacity to solve academic problems. In Lebanon, each school has a PEBLS team that meets on a regular basis to review schoolwide and individual data regarding student achievement. The teams look at the entire range of data regarding students including absences, behavior, attitude, skills, and disabilities to determine why students are not being successful academically. Student failure is systemic. For that reason, we must build *systems* that influence the causes for student failure rather than continually treating the symptoms.

The Director of Student Achievement oversees the PEBLS teams throughout the district and has invested a great deal of time and energy into training these teams to have the capacity to solve the problems that are leading to student failure. As a result, each PEBLS team has identified a standard set of both academic and behavior interventions its school has found to be successful in meeting the majority of student needs. These teams help identify and target students that are struggling before they get so far behind they qualify for special education. The PEBLS teams throughout the district meet together twice a year at a PEBLS conference to share with other schools their successful interventions. In this way, capacity is built from school to school because nothing is more powerful than teachers sharing with teachers what is and is not working to meet student needs.

THE POWER OF COMMUNITY TO BUILD CAPACITY

Capacity-building refers to activities that improve the community's ability to achieve the school's vision or an individual's ability to do a job more effectively. The whole order of things within the school will be changed when the principal moves from problem-solving to capacity-building and the followers move from learned helplessness to active problem-solving. The impact on the workforce is tremendous. A new vitality and resilience will emerge when workers feel empowered and competent to resolve problems interdependently. The leader will be freed to promote the school's vision and progress will be made.

Capacity-building as a concept focuses not only on the skills and capabilities of the individuals within a school but also with the collective's ability to achieve its vision effectively and to sustain itself over the long haul. It is the collective that provides the greatest opportunity to build capacity. In today's parlance the collective is better described as the school community.

A community has at least five attributes that define its existence. A sense of community among all of its members that reflects these five qualities creates a climate for capacity-building within a school or district. The five attributes are:

1. A sense of belonging to the group.
2. The acknowledgment of each member's mutual importance by each member of the group.
3. The profession of common beliefs, which include shared values and strong emotional ties.
4. The networking or bonding through frequent interactions.
5. The acceptance of the mutual responsibility for sustaining positive interrelationships within the group.

If a solitary hero-leader solves all the school or district's problems, the sense of belonging to the group is reduced. The importance of the members is lessened. Problem-solving as a group concern and activity is lost. The need to get together to wrestle with the problem is removed. And finally, the responsibility for one another is shifted to one individual. If, however, a leader spends more time developing these five attributes of community then greater problem-solving capacity can be achieved. The issue of capacity is critical to a leader's reform agenda. Without the capabilities and desire to act on the part of the members of a school community very little will be achieved.

DEVELOPING SOCIAL CAPITAL

Capacity-building is twofold. First, it is the development of awareness, skills, knowledge, motivation, commitment, resilience, and confidence within each member of the community. Second, it is the development of social capital. Social capital in this case is the increased level of networking, social cohesion, and communication that is operative within the community. It might be best described as the formation of an alliance among the community's entire membership. This would create a credible group of individuals who strive to benefit all of the members of the group in some way. In organizations with high levels of social capital, it is all for one and one for all. Everyone strives to engage issues, problems, and opportunities so that the community's vision can be realized. Sergiovanni (1994) explains it this way, "The need for community is universal. A sense of belonging, of continuity, of being connected to others and to ideas and values that make our lives meaningful and significant—these needs are shared by all of us" (p. xiii).

Broad-based skillful involvement of the members of the school community is a powerful means by which the group can weather the ever-present challenges that encircle school districts today. The involvement described here underscores two key facets, the breadth of involvement and the skillfulness with which the members undertake their work. When the capacity of the staff is fully built out, the leadership within the school is no longer identified only with the designated leaders. This condition establishes the resilience to withstand changes in designated leadership positions and keeps the effects of change more constructive for those affected by them.

EFFECTIVE REFORM HINGES ON BUILDING CAPACITY

There is much to be said about the type of system that we are attempting to reform in education today. If we view schools from a mechanistic perspective we tend to replace parts or tinker with the tuning of the apparatus like curriculum, instruction, or personnel. We make one change at a time and then evaluate the effect that the change has had on the system. This is quite linear in nature. In that reform model we are simply repairing the conveyor belt in the education factory.

If, however, we view schools and districts as living systems, we begin by considering the health and vitality of the system and then treating it as a whole. These two approaches reveal the essence of the issue. Problem-solving is associated with a more mechanistic view of change while capacity-building is a strategy that furthers the health and vitality of a living system. Education is a people business and relationships are paramount to quality community development. These are characteristics of a living system. Thus, capacity-building enables a living system to adapt and change for its own benefit and by so doing it maintains its health and vitality.

The linear model of school reform is outdated and ineffective. There is no silver bullet curriculum or charismatic leader who can solve all of the problems, and there is no amount of contrived accountability that can make schools do better. NCLB will fail not because the concept is bad. It will fail because it addresses reform as a mechanism rather than a system. Educators want all of their children to succeed. No principal points kids out for failure and decides to leave them behind. The current structure of NCLB counts the number of kids that fail—cut-and-dry. Take the tests and count the failures.

A systemic model of reform would not look at yearly failures along pre-determined, arbitrary cut-offs, but *how long* it took each child to reach the agreed upon standards. In that kind of system, no child would be left behind. Each one would get what they needed (time and specific instruction) to reach the next benchmark of learning. In Lebanon's continuous progress model, students take the appropriate test when they are ready and proceed to the next level of instruction accordingly. This model has resulted in significant test score improvements over the past seven years when compared to state averages.

Our improvements are not indicative of a linear or prescribed model of reform, but a systemic view of improvement that focuses on building a teacher's capacity for instruction. The student improvement results we have seen in Lebanon are more closely related to the teachers' *commitment* to a curriculum rather than any one particular curriculum. Our teachers use a combination of direct and discovery instructional methods, phonetics and whole language, project-based and packet-driven teaching that centers around one single question: what does this child need?

Since we have no predetermined path for our reform to go, we have moved beyond the linear, top-down models that only last as long as the person or grant that made everyone do it. In our model of reform, the system itself increases in its capacity to solve its own problems. Improvement and growth are therefore simply by-products of our increased capacity.

BUILDING CAPACITY VIA SMALL LEARNING COMMUNITIES

The high school reform movement toward small learning communities has received national attention and funding from both public and private sources. The research is in Littky (2004), Sizer (1984), and Howley and Harmon (2000). In general, smaller schools demonstrate higher rates of academic and behavioral success because student needs are known. Relationships are maximized, and when students are known through the power of relationships, they are more successful in every way. In large schools, principals can build capacity by creating smallness through teachers teaming together in benchmark, interest, or family groupings. The key is not how smallness is created—just that it is done.

After Lebanon received grants to create small learning communities in their large high school, they created a leadership team to manage the funds and implement the reform. On the leadership team, all members had equal standing, and the team had ultimate authority on what changes to make and how to instigate them. The leadership team effectively increased the capacity of the building to solve problems because more people on every level of the organization became responsible for its success, and though the grant funding was temporary, the capacity generated from a leadership team without hierarchy endured. Shared decision-making and ownership for those decisions became a reality.

A VISION FOR CAPACITY

What are the distinguishing characteristics of the living system we call school when it is healthy and vital? In Lebanon, we have by no means arrived, but we have a heightened sense of bearing after seven years. In a high capacity system, people reflect on their work and collaboratively construct meaning and make sense of their efforts. A spirit of experimentation and inquiry is prevalent within the school community. Conversations are progressive and anticipatory where future innovations are developed. These conversations, reflections, and inquiries lead to actions that are intentional and based upon renewing the mental constructs around the work within the school community.

People are willing to engage conflict that inevitably arises when risk-taking is present in the community. This collective spirit produces a synergy that secures the well-being of the community itself. These characteristics establish an embedded kind of leadership that is not vested in selected individuals but is engaged by all members of the community as an attribute available to all who develop it rather than those upon whom it might be bestowed. And finally, the climate within the community is positive and laced with humor because the members truly enjoy being a part of this living system called school.

At Pioneer School in Lebanon, we've had the pleasure of watching the birth of a healthy community with high levels of capacity. Representatives from another district had visited to see first hand how signature schools functioned and how our continuous progress model of learning existed within the strict confines of grade levels and yearly testing. Dr. Hess's teaching staff was circled in the library discussing all of the innovative ways the system is altered in order to meet student needs. The visiting district kept asking the same questions again and again—almost in disbelief that a staff of teachers could be so accommodating to student needs. Finally one of Pioneer's teachers just said, "The kids are different every year. You have to change what you are doing to meet their needs. What else would you do?" When everything has been done, there is nothing left to do. In a continuous progress model, it is impossible to do everything. Change becomes the constant. Innovation is expected. Improvement is the outcome.

BUILDING CAPACITY AS LIVING SYSTEMS

According to Margaret Wheatley, three conditions must be present for living systems to build capacity as an entire community. The interaction of purpose, relationships, and information play a powerful role in the growth of the organization or community. The restructuring begins with developing capacity for an organization or community to reach a greater level of self-awareness. In Wheatley's own words:

> My colleagues and I focus on helping a system develop greater self-knowledge in three critical areas. People need to be connected to the fundamental identity of the organization or community. Who are we? Who do we aspire to become? How shall we be together? And people need to be connected to new information. What else do we need to know? Where is this new information to be found? And people need to be able to reach past traditional boundaries and develop relationship with people anywhere in the system. Who else needs to be here to do this work with us? (Wheatley 1999, p. 146)

As we help an organization to build capacity in their vision, the system will reorganize, change, and become a completely different system. Problems will disappear because the root causes will have disappeared. Priority leaders treat causes, not symptoms. They intervene to redesign the system to dissolve problems rather than just hide them with weak or temporary solutions. The system redesign is best generated from the inside-out rather than by the hero-leader who will use the outside-in path. Systems change starts with the attention we pay to purpose, relationships, and new information. These are not a linear progression. It happens simultaneously. It is the interaction of these parts that produces the sparks.

PURPOSE-DRIVEN TO BUILD CAPACITY

To build capacity, people must become more aware and connected to the purpose of the organization. Only the individuals can decide if the change is necessary for the good of themselves and the organization. No amount of external pressure can alter this fact. Workers can be persuaded, directed, and ordered, but true commitment to the organizational purpose and any changes that must occur can only effectively come at the individual level.

As individuals truly connect with the purpose of the organization their individual identity or purpose will begin to integrate. "Any living thing will change only if it sees change as a means of preserving itself" (Wheatley 1999). This is true of individuals and organizations. Connecting with the organizational purpose is just one step in the right direction. Offering people the mirror to see themselves both individually and organizationally still requires two more aspects of relationships and new information.

THE POWER OF NEW INFORMATION

New information becomes vital as organizations struggle with their identity. It is critical that leaders help people find the right questions that attach to the identity or purpose of the organization. The problem solver rarely stops long enough to "question the questions" but rushes forward to "find the answer" and feed the expectations of the followers. Some would call this job security. In reality, it is the slow death of the organization. Priority leaders take time to question the questions. They reflect on the processes, and more importantly, they teach others to reflect and question the questions. They question everything.

With questions come data and new information. New information must come from a diverse number of places. Hero-leaders make the mistake of being the only information source. It is a source of power. It is like the teacher in the traditional classroom that is perceived as the dispenser of knowledge. Students come to expect that the teacher will take care of them. The teacher will decide what is important and what is not important. The teacher will decide who has the right answers and who does not. The teacher has a death grip on the information pipeline and so it is in most organizations. It is an expectation that began in the classroom.

The capacity builder must break this cycle. We must teach others to find answers for themselves. We must teach them how to fish rather than just giving them the fish. The art of questioning must be consciously taught to everyone in the organization. Questioning is the heart of reflection, and there is a strong body of research that has linked reflection to effective instruction (Jay 2003). The priority leader develops system infrastructure that supports time for organizational and individual reflection and conversation. Common planning times, collaborative inquiry protocols, staff retreats, periodic sustained and focused professional development activities are just a few examples.

Jay (2003) writes about three types of reflection: reflection-on-action, reflection-in-action, and reflection-for-action. Reflection-on-action involves pausing after an activity to see how it went, and asking what went well, what didn't, and what could be improved.

Reflection-in-action (Schon 1983, 1987) occurs when someone changes direction in the midst of an activity. Teachers do this when they change a lesson because the class is no longer paying attention or they try a new approach because the students didn't grasp the concept as presented. Great teachers constantly reflect-in-action.

Reflection-for-action (Killion and Todnem 1991) begins with a thought that will lead to further actions. It is forward thinking brainstorming that is not based on trying to improve activity that has already passed but to begin a new activity that hasn't been tried yet.

All three reflective activities are grounded in questions and result in new information. Priority leaders employ activities that support reflection including "journal writing, portfolio creation, conversations with colleagues, evaluations of practice, reflective interviews, peer observations, group seminars, video-tapes of practice, analysis of practice according to standards, and analysis of student work" (Jay 2003, p. 19).

RELATIONSHIPS BUILD CAPACITY

Relationships are the riverways for the flow of new information. The fundamental element in the living system model is the relationship between two or more people. Rene Descartes once stated, "I think, there-fore I am." The equivalent for organizations or communities can be found in the African statement, "I see you, therefore you exist." Our ex-istence depends on others. We are "interdependent" beings—not "in-dependent" beings we sometimes profess. We are who we are through our interactions with others. There is no greater crime in education to-day than the extreme sense of isolationism we have created in the very infrastructure of our school day. We force teachers to teach in isolation. Class sizes continue to increase. We herd children through classrooms with barely enough time to sit down before we move them to the next teacher. We squeeze out our planning time and collaboration is nearly non-existent. At best we have some common planning time but little or no protocols to facilitate effective collaboration, reflection, or conversa-tion. The simple act of conversation is a monumental task in most schools today.

Wheatley (1999) argues we must connect all parts of the organization to itself. Isolationism not only exists on an individual scale, but organi-zationally as well. Schools rarely collaborate. Teachers from different levels rarely talk to one another. When was the last time a kindergarten teacher spent time with a high school teacher? Classified staff is left out of most conversations. Schedules, policies, and procedures are the cul-prits in most cases. District office personnel often feel isolated from the real conversations that are happening at the building level. Parents and community members are often frustrated by the lack of conversation that comes their way. At best they may receive a weekly newsletter that has little value for any real level of engagement.

Creating genuine engaging relationships with all stakeholders is a major task for any leader who seeks to build capacity. Problem solvers ignore this aspect and simply look for the solutions that the leader hopes will make everyone happy. Many times these are solutions to problems spawned by isolationism. Once satisfied, followers cherish their leader and ask for more and more help. The ego of the problem-solving leader is never sufficiently fed, and the cycle continues until the organization is so leader dependent it will collapse when the leader exits or can no longer keep up with the amount of problems that continue to surface. Leadership burnout is in-evitable. Once gone, the organization will demand another problem solver and the cycle continues. Organizational death soon follows.

To battle the pull of isolationism in Lebanon schools, we have created collaborative teams of educators that reflect together on their practice on a regular basis. By formally training teacher leaders as mentors and critical friends group (CFG) leaders and requiring teachers to become a part of collegial teams as a component of their professional growth, we have created a structure for reflection to occur.

CONCLUSION: MOVING FROM PROBLEM-SOLVING TO CAPACITY-BUILDING

Priority leaders are constantly looking for ways to build capacity in their followers. They accomplish this in a variety of ways: reflection, delegation, empowerment, relationships, and intrinsic motivation. They resist stepping in to solve problems and seek to improve the system so that the people in it are engaged to solve the problems and look for opportunities for improvement. Priority leaders do not stress over minor problems that surface. They are constantly looking at the big picture and discovering the causes that influence the problems. They address the system, not the symptoms.

5

FROM ISOLATION AND FEAR OF SEPARATION TO RELATIONSHIPS AND TEAMWORK

Collaboration improves performance . . . and such collaboration (teacher to teacher) is our most effective tool for improving instruction.

Mike Schmoker

Esprit de corps is a oneness of spirit that confirms the vision and priorities of an organization through relationships and connections. In high performing schools the working environment is supportive and fun-filled. It is marked by strong levels of trust, openness, sharing, and ownership. Research on successful companies has unearthed the fact that members of companies that achieve breakthrough results have fun together. They actually enjoy meeting together and look for ways to spend time with each other beyond the workplace (Collins 2001).

After several years of successful business, Max De Pree (1997) became more and more convinced that competence in relationships was at the heart of all organizations. Educator and reformer Roland Barth (2001) boldly makes the following claim: "I learned over and over again that the relationship among the adults in the schoolhouse has more impact on the quality and character of the school—and the accomplishment of youngsters—than any other factor" (p. 105). He couldn't be more correct. Effective organizations have oneness, a community that binds people together through thick and thin. They constantly stick up for one another, support each other, and go to bat for each other.

Combat soldiers are known for their oneness and unity because their very lives and survival are dependent on those around them. They must trust and support each other. That is why the armed services are so attractive for young men and women. However, in the world of work, we can easily survive without having to depend on anyone but ourselves. The notion of rugged individualism and charismatic leaders that can do it all only perpetuates the separation. Organizations don't become great that way. As a matter of fact, Collins (2001) discovered that the talented, charismatic leaders were not the ones running companies that made the jump from good to great He found again and again that it was the hard-working, determined, humble, dedicated ones committed for the long haul that were leading the transformation to greatness.

RELATIONSHIPS GENERATE RESULTS

In Patrick Lencioni's leadership fable *The Five Dysfunctions of a Team* (2002), he makes the claim that teamwork is vehicle through which greatness is achieved. "If you could get all the people in an organization rowing in the same direction, you could dominate any industry, in any market, against any competition" (Lencioni 2002, p. vii). Lencioni outlines a clear trail from teamwork to results, and he distills teamwork to the foundation of trust—in other words, relationship. He states that trust is established through vulnerability and the willingness to share weaknesses and admit mistakes.

Robbins (2005) maintains that trust is sustained by putting the interests of others ahead of your own. Once trust is established, teams have the confidence and courage to engage in the meaningful exchange of ideas—that will naturally cause conflict. The willingness to embrace conflict and work through it enables a team to commit to group decisions without engaging in parking lot backstabbing. Committing actions based on group decisions leads team members toward holding each other accountable—not only for their work assignments, but also for their behavior on the team. The ability to hold one another accountable to their actions without resentment will naturally lead to powerful, measurable results.

Michael Roberto, author of *Why Great Leaders Don't Take Yes for an Answer* (2005), agrees with the importance of constructive conflict as a necessary ingredient for success, and also emphasizes the importance of surfacing that conflict:

> Leaders need to recognize that expressing dissent can be very difficult and uncomfortable for lower-level managers and employees. Therefore, leaders cannot wait for dissent to come to them: they must actively *go seek it out* in their organizations. In short, they must search for people willing to say no to them.

To facilitate the process of constructive conflict, leaders need to develop a variety of forums and ways team members can express their views. Working through conflict helps to build decision-commitment, which in the long run will lead to a greater implementation of ideas.

THE POWER OF TEAMWORK ON THE FOOTBALL FIELD

In an age of free agency and financial caps that has effectively made parity widespread throughout the National Football League, the New England Patriots are one of the few teams that have constantly been at the top at the turn of the millennium, and they are the only team successful enough in recent years to engage the "dynasty" question. Why? What sets them apart? One word: team.

Just about every football fan knows the story of the Patriots who demonstrate every weekend the triumph of team over individual egos. Their strategy for success is not the signing of big name stars, but instead recognizing underutilized talent, signing potential, and then training the recruit to play a part in the system. They have the confidence and ability year after year to promote from within and not miss a beat (Zimmerman 2005).

Their march to the 2005 Super Bowl brought the high-scoring Indianapolis Colts to their doorstep. The same Colts who averaged over 30 points a game with Peyton Manning throwing a record 49 touchdown passes. The doubters thought the Patriots might just be out of steam. Their secondary was depleted by injuries, and Manning's Colts were on a roll. When a courageous reporter asked Patriot coach Bill Belichick how they could possibly stop the Colts without their star cornerback, Ty Law, Belichick responded smartly, "One guy can't stop the Colts. No, you have to do it as a team" (Silver 2005, p. 40). And that's exactly what they did—pounding the Colts 20–3.

In the 2005 season they grounded the best air attack in the league (Colts), and then turned around the next week to drill the best ground game (Steelers) into the turf, 41–27. The Patriots discovered the power of teamwork to overcome all obstacles, and never became one dimensional. Through teamwork they were able to beat the most successful passing and running teams on successive weekends. Constantly applying the principles of team-first they have consistently found themselves on top of the standings.

At their first Super Bowl success in 2002 they refused to be individually introduced while taking on the St. Louis Rams. It was more than a gimmick. They'd been doing it for over half the season. The Patriots entered that game 14-point underdogs and walked away with the Lombardi trophy. No one gave them a chance to win it, but they believed—not just in themselves but in each other.

To build the most effective team of the new millennium, coach Bill Belichick and his staff looked at over 200 free agents in the spring of 2001. They signed 17 of them for a combined $2.7 million—small change in today's high priced sports market of name brand superstars. While the rest of the league was looking for that one great player who could turn a team around, Belichick was quietly building a team—and that team did turn it all around. A year after going 5–11 in 2001, they stormed back to win a Super Bowl against the mighty, high-flying Rams in 2002.

When the Patriots quietly looked for players during that fateful spring, they scouted not just hidden talent, but constantly and consistently looked for team guys—players who would make the locker room a better place to be—ones that would support others and make them better. The mentality of team over stardom was never more apparent then in Belichick's benching of All Pro quarterback Drew Bledsoe in favor of the young and unproven Tom Brady in the middle of that turnaround season. Belichick was criticized and second-guessed by the savvy Boston fans for weeks because of the move.

In spite of the pressure, Belichick stuck with his ultimate team player, and when Brady held the Lombardi trophy over his head that January all was quiet on the Eastern front. Winners don't get second-guessed. They get praised for being innovative and "thinking outside the box." The no-nonsense, team-oriented Tom Brady began his career as an unheralded seventh round draft pick. He also began it by winning more postseason games consecutively than any other quarterback. The 2005 Super Bowl victory gave him 10 in a row.

THE WORLD OF PROFIT AND NON-PROFIT: WINNING AND LOSING

Team sports are the ultimate results-orientated business. Every outing is marked down as a success or failure by one simple factor—did you win or lose? Individuals can have great games, but if the team loses, the individual loses as well. In the world of business, winning and losing also comes down to one factor—profit. Is the company making money or not? Are you gaining on your competitors or losing ground? Companies that don't continually find ways to make money don't exist very long into the future.

In the non-profit world, however, there is no clear defining scoreboard. Take education, for example. Is there one element that defines a winning educational team? Is it test scores? Attendance? Hours of volunteers in the school? Years of experience in a teaching staff? Number of teachers with master's degrees? Number of students suspended? Number of students going on to education after high school? What makes a winning school? Is there such a thing and should we be trying to create winners and losers in education? Perhaps NCLB will define winners and losers via AYP ratings, but educators are not in agreement that such rankings actually improve the nature of teaching and learning in schools.

We all agree that schools can be better, and maybe that's the purpose of NCLB. But just what do we mean by better? The non-profit world of schools, churches, and other organizations do not define success by winning or losing, or making a profit. In the non-profit world we can only define success via quality: quality of product *and* quality of experience.

QUALITY OF PRODUCT AND QUALITY OF EXPERIENCE

Quality of product can be easily measured and compared across organizations. For instance, in the world of schools, quality of product indicators would be attendance rates, test score achievement, number of teachers with advanced degrees, instructional days, hours of instruction per day, hours of small group instruction, and dozens of other items that can be easily measured and compared.

The same concept would apply to quality of product indicators in churches. Churches would look at the number of members, number of visitors, number of conversions throughout the year, etc. Since quality of product indictors are easily measured and compared, they often become the basis for outsiders to judge the results of what is happening in schools and other non-profits. However, for those who are *inside* those organizations and members of them, *quality of experience* indicators are the most valuable measurements.

In the non-profit world, quality of experience matters. For most if not all parents, it is more important that their children come home with smiles on their faces beaming about how much fun they had in school, the friends they made, that their teachers are nice and helpful, and what they learned than whether their local school got a "satisfactory" or "strong" on the state report card rating last year.

Quality of experience levels cannot be gleaned from test scores, attendance logs, or computer screens. Quality of experience can only be determined by interacting with the people having the experience through interviews, surveys, or observations. It takes much more time to measure and is harder to compare quality of experience values, but for organizations (especially non-profits) wishing to improve their services, it is critical to engage quality of experience measurements to determine what matters to their clients and how they can deliver on those values.

QUALITY OF EXPERIENCE CAN DRIVE PROFIT

As a matter of fact, more and more for-profit businesses are discovering that quality of experience is a key driver to repeat customers, brand loyalty and eventual bottom-line results. Nordstrom's is one of the most well-known retail outlets to base their entire philosophy on providing a quality experience for every customer who walks in the door. From simple directives such as "The customer is always right," to giving floor sales people the authority to make decisions regarding pricing and other extras to please the customer, they have built a tradition of service and customer base so loyal people go out of their way to shop at Nordstrom's. Every loyal Nordstrom's customer has a "Nordstrom's story" to tell, and others who have only heard about the legendary service venture into their stores just to see if it is true.

Quality of experience has a direct correlation to improved relationships. Higher levels of quality, money, or wins in the standings can all be connected to positive relationships which only happen through highly functioning teams. Since teamwork is so strongly correlated to results, it almost seems like ineffective teams are more prevalent in the non-profit world. It is easier to have ineffective teams and relationships in the non-profit world because no one is keeping score—officially.

POSITIVE RELATIONSHIPS BEGIN WITH TRUST

Relationships hinge on trust. When trust is absent, there is fear and further separation. People become territorial, selfish, and ego-driven. In an environment of fear, trust is non-existent. "It requires team members to make themselves vulnerable to one another, and be confident that their respective vulnerabilities will not be used against them. The vulnerabilities include weaknesses, skill deficiencies, interpersonal shortcomings, mistakes, and requests for help" (Lencioni 2002, p. 196). Without vulnerability-based trust, there is no relationship. In a trust-filled environment people can have tough accountability discussions that will foster improvement as opposed to constantly looking out for their own interests and career advancement.

The foundation of trust is not developed overnight. Many school boards are under the false impression that great improvement and results can only be achieved by bringing in someone from the outside to "shake things up," and get everyone motivated. However, "the evidence does not support the idea that you need an outside leader to come in and shake up the place to go from good to great. In fact, going for a high profile outside change agent is *negatively correlated* with a sustained transformation from good to great" (Collins 2001, p. 31).

In other words, new flashy leaders who want to change everything in order to prove why they are worth their salaries have a greater tendency to cause fear of separation rather than building relationships. It takes time and effort to build relationships. It doesn't happen overnight. Organizations that go for the quick transformation rather than build teamwork and relationships with sustained priorities over time are always disappointed and underachieving with the talent they have on hand.

RELATIONSHIPS: THE NEW GIFT ECONOMY

There is a new business model on the horizon. "The more you give away, the more you have" (Rubin 1999, p. 330). In this new model, generosity, not greed, is a strategic good. In 1998 Don Norman left Hewlett Packard to work solo, and he is in the business of putting people in connection with people. In his book *The Design of Everyday Things* (1998), he lists his 10,000 contacts in his PDA as his most significant asset. His philosophy is simple: the more he helps people make connections with others to build businesses, the bigger and stronger his network becomes, and the more benefits return to him.

The gift economy is based on the idea that gifts are a means of currency, not property. A gift must be circulated. The term "Indian giver" exemplifies the story behind the gift economy. When Indians gave settlers a gift, they expected one in return. Instead of keeping gifts in circulation, the settlers would put the peace pipes they received on their mantles. The Indians believed gifts were meant to be kept in circulation. When they didn't get something in return, they asked for their gifts back. This shocked the settlers and their traditional notions of property. The settlers faulted the Indians for their bad manners, but to the Indians, it was just good economics (Rubin 1999). Relationships are central to the gift economy. Effective leaders invest in relationships knowing that the energy spent in time, favors, and gifts will yield dividends of success that will reach far and wide.

THE SOUTHWEST AIRLINES MIRACLE: RELATIONSHIPS IN ACTION

For a trip to San Francisco, Dr. Hess needed to call the Southwest Airlines help phone number a few times about a rental car and flight departure times. Every time he called, the phone was answered within a couple of rings. No help lines, no working your way through complicated automated menus. Finally, he noticed the pattern and asked the helpful, cheerful airline phone worker how she did it: "How can my calls get picked up so quickly?" He expected an answer like, "We're trained to do it," or "We hire a lot of people to answer phones." What she said shocked him: "We've been waiting here all night for you to call."

When it comes to business success and job satisfaction, few organizations can top the phenomenon of Southwest Airlines. Southwest is the only airline to have won the industry's "Triple Crown": the fewest delays, the fewest complaints, and the fewest mishandled bags—not only for individual months but for entire years, from 1992 through 1996. No other airline has won the honor for more than one month at a time. Southwest is also known for its record levels of safety. They have never suffered a fatality (unlike any other major airline), and they have the fewest pilot deviations per flight departure of all major airlines (Gittell 2003). Southwest does more than just keep customers happy due to their safety and service. They are also the only airline to post a profit every year for over 30 years. They have only been in operation since 1967, and during the first six months of 2004, Southwest employed over 34,000 people and flew more domestic passengers than any other airline. Without question, they are the quintessential example of a company that is achieving high levels of quality of product and experience. The company is making money, and the customers are happy. They keep coming back.

Southwest has grown at a nearly constant rate of 10 to 15 percent every year. It is unusual and powerful when an organizational practice results in both increased quality and increased efficiency. Their remarkable success has turned the head of every airline and countless other companies who are trying to discover the "Southwest Secret." And to the surprise of all, Southwest doesn't mind sharing—even with competitors! They conduct conferences every year where others can learn about how Southwest does business, and the world is a happier, more productive place because of their generosity.

Author Judy Gittell spent 8 years researching Southwest and other airlines to discover Southwest's secret to success. She discovered that Southwest's most powerful organizational competency is its ability to build and sustain high performance relationships between managers, employees, unions, and suppliers. Southwest sees these internal and external relationships not only as a success factor, "but as the most *essential* success factor. They believe that to develop the company, they must constantly invest in relationships" (Gittell 2003, p. 266). She goes on to say that "with strong relationships, employees embrace rather than reject their connections with one another, enabling them to coordinate more effectively with each other" (p. 35).

Most people understand the need and value of positive relationships. So what is the big deal with Southwest? The big deal is that they *really* believe it, and they live it out. From day one in 1967, co-founding CEO Herb Kelleher invited the unions in to Southwest. He believed not only that management could have a positive relationship with hard-core unions, but that the strength of that relationship would make his company *better*. Kelleher used the presence of unions as a balance of power in his organization to make sure management didn't use their power and authority in corrupt ways.

Thirty years later, he is beginning to convert the skeptics. Southwest is the most heavily unionized airline in the country with more than 85 percent of their workforce members of unions. By the same token, they have the quickest time-to-contract rating in the industry, and the fewest work stoppages—only one strike (6 days) in over 30 years—unheard of in the airline industry. Since 1985 they have had only two mediations and arbitrations. Employees are happy and working relationships between management and employees run so smoothly that analysts have made the assumption that Southwest is a union-free operation and erroneously attributed *a lack of unions* as a reason for their success (Gittell 2003).

Since the beginning, Herb Kelleher operated from the belief that if the company took care of its employees, then they would take care of the company. By making the workplace like a family, Southwest has learned how to gain the loyalty and commitment of its employees at a deep level. When Southwest hires, they hire for relational competency. They promote from within, and once someone makes it through their difficult probation period, they keep who they hire. After 9/11, the airline industry averaged an 18 percent workforce reduction just to survive. Southwest continued to operate like a family, not laying off anyone. Herb always thought the short-term profit to be made via layoffs would eventually hurt long-term success. Kelleher explained his philosophy regarding layoffs in early 2001 before the 9/11 crisis hit:

> Nothing kills your company's culture like layoffs. Nobody has ever been furloughed [at Southwest], and that is unprecedented in the airline industry. It's been a huge strength of ours. It's certainly helped us negotiate our union contracts. We could have furloughed at various times and been more profitable, but I always thought that was shortsighted. You want to show your people that you value them and you're not going to hurt them just to get a little more money in the short term. Not furloughing people breeds loyalty. It breeds a sense of security. It breeds a sense of trust. So in bad times you take care of them and in good times they're thinking, perhaps, "We've never lost our jobs. That's a pretty good reason to stick around." (Gittell 2003, p. 243)

After 9/11, Herb was proven right again. Southwest didn't lay anyone off during the crisis, and within a year, they had recovered routes and passengers in areas where other airlines had cut back. One of the keys to making relationships work in an organization is to develop credibility. Credibility comes by telling it straight for long enough that people come to trust what you say, but it must be clear to your employees that their top leadership cares deeply about their well-being (Gittell 2003). If this is not the case, strong relationships will be hard to forge.

GAME THEORY APPLIED

The power of relationships to achieve the best possible results for all sides is an application of *game theory,* popularized recently by Ron Howard's Best Picture–winning film, *A Beautiful Mind.* The film was based on the biography of mathematician John Forbes Nash Jr., written by Sylvia Nasar in 1998.

It was in the 1950s that the 21-year-old Nash brought to game theory a new twist—the possibility of win-win. He was the first to theorize that in a competitive situation, cooperation can be added in order to discover the equilibrium where all players can walk away satisfied as winners with a collective result that is superior to what either side could have achieved on their own (Nasar 1998). The remarkable result of Southwest CEO Herb Kelleher's cooperative work in the competitive, cutthroat world of unions is an example of Nash's theory in action. *The Southwest Way* (Gittell 2003) documents the dominance of Southwest Airlines based on the simple yet profound theory that pursuing and achieving positive relationships between all parties is the foundation of success.

Dr. Hess's earlier book *Excellence, Equity, and Efficiency* (2005) documents the competitive forces that exist between the values of excellence, equity, and efficiency in the world of education. He proposes a framework, the Quality School Improvement Framework, for achieving the equilibrium or *cooperation* among these intensely competitive forces. It is precisely in finding the right relationships among these values that breakthrough results can be achieved.

The inverse is true as well—in a cooperative situation, competition can be added to achieve greater results for everyone. Take, for example, a simple schoolwide canned food drive. Without exception, when competition between classrooms for the most food returned is added, the collective food drive will yield a greater result.

Nash demonstrated the power of relationships in other ways as well. He was not a loner. Even though he was competitive, he was remarkably good at getting other people to join in his projects. At MIT, Nash completed his most important work by persuading half a dozen colleagues to spend months collaborating with him to complete his proof (Nasar 1998). He realized that cooperation through relationships was a central component to succeed in a competitive environment. In 1994 Nash was awarded the Nobel peace prize for his breakthrough game theory concepts that ending up finding applications throughout the business and education world. In the magical world of relationships, the sum of the whole is greater than the total of the parts, and separation through isolation only creates winners, losers, and a shallow bottom line.

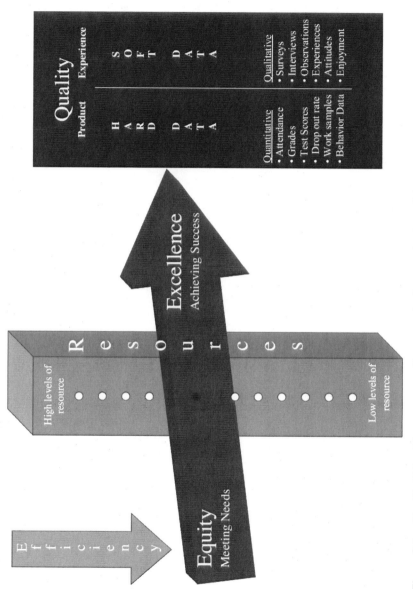

Figure 5.1. Quality School Improvement Framework: A systemic view of the interaction between excellence, equity, and efficiency and its effect on quality.

THE IMPORTANCE OF HUMOR

Laughter is the shortest distance between two people.

Sebastian Bach

Humor builds relationships—providing you are not tearing down others for amusement. A 3,000-year-old proverb states that laughter is good medicine, and now we can prove it. Recent brain research is revealing that the entire brain, and therefore the body, is affected in a positive way when people laugh. There is a circuit that runs throughout the brain that produces laughter. Whereas other emotions just focus on certain areas of the brain, laughter is dependent entirely upon relationships throughout the brain. Laughter shuts off the flow of stress hormones and suppresses the flight and fight compounds that are based in fear. When we're laughing, natural cells that destroy tumors and viruses are released (AATH 2004). Keeping loose before big events is essential, and often humor is used to keep people sane in times of stress, worry, and trouble. "Humor creates social bonds" (Trout 1998), and social bonds build relationships.

Abraham Lincoln was known for this sense of humor during the most trying of times. History once records him reading a book of humor during a dark and bloody phase of the Civil War to his cabinet members and laughing. He admonished the leaders by saying, "Gentlemen, why don't you laugh? If I should not laugh, I would die, and you need this medicine as much as I do." Remember this piece of advice is coming from a man whose life was marred by one setback after another including failed businesses, political defeats, bouts with depression, the death of three sons and his wife—not to mention the stress and pressure of trying to hold a country together that was in the grip of the most bloody and grisly war of our nation's history (Klein 1988).

Humor unites people to a common cause. It dispels fear and builds relationships, unity, and teamwork. In most high performance organizations, you will find people laughing, having a good time, enjoying themselves—and working hard. Effective leaders use humor to build relationships and teamwork and dispel stress and the fear of separation.

CONCLUSION: MOVING FROM ISOLATION AND FEAR OF SEPARATION TO RELATIONSHIPS AND TEAMWORK

Judith Viorst, novelist and poet, has written,

> Just as children, step by step, must separate from their parents, we will have to separate from them. And we will probably suffer . . . from some degree of separation anxiety: because separation ends sweet symbiosis. Because separation reduces our power and control. Because separation makes us feel less needed, less important. And because separation exposes our children to danger. (1986)

Viorst has described one of many separations we experience throughout our lives. Even in the best of situations a little of our hearts is taken from us when we experience separation. We do develop anxiety over the sense of loss that separation creates. The transition from childhood to adulthood is a necessary separation from parental authority to the new relationships that are created when young adults begin to form their own families. It is not so much a losing of childhood as it is gaining responsibility through adulthood.

Staying connected in the work environment is important to our sense of well-being and our desire to share our work with one another. It is time for priority leaders to tear down walls of separation and engage in the creation of opportunities for relationship building among the workers within the system. Leaders should refrain from using the threats of separation (dismissals, transfers) to manage the organization. These separations may be necessary from time to time but they should not hang heavy over the organization in such a way that separation anxiety prevents the workers from maximizing their innovative efforts. Breakthrough improvement comes through teamwork and relationships. It is rarely achieved through separation and isolation.

6

FROM CONTROLLING MANAGERS TO SHARED LEADERSHIP

The best executive is one who has the sense enough to pick good men to do what he wants done, and the self-restraint enough to keep from meddling with them while they do it.

Theodore Roosevelt

Controlling managers in schools seek compliance from their subordinates. They operate in the world of mistrust and coercion. They understand the importance of outcomes and control as much of the process as possible. They spend a great deal of time in teacher observations, writing reports, and conducting meetings designed to improve the areas of weakness they discover. As a result, they write many "plans of assistance" because they are serious about improvement, and they want to get it right. Unfortunately, their efforts to control will succeed. They will develop compliant teachers who will work hard to "stay in line" and not rock the boat. They will also develop environments resistant to change where few will innovate or take any risks. They will create workplaces where teachers will wonder whether they are behaving "right." Their goal will be to stay out of trouble. They will comply, and when the school underperforms, the controlling manager will point fingers and blame their weak teaching staff, insufficient resources, or "bad demographics" for the poor results.

Sharing leaders embrace ownership. They seek commitment from their staff members. Unlike controlling managers, they realize they are responsible for outcomes, and they know intuitively that the most effective outcomes are not possible without commitment from all staff members. For this reason, they *do not* focus on the process. All of their energy is directed at the outcomes, and they give their staff members the liberty and resources to pursue those outcomes as they choose. People get what they seek. Commitment cannot be mandated. An employee can only willingly give commitment. It is internal, and when leaders provide an environment free of fear and full of trust and support, most workers will eventually commit to the cause—and they will enjoy working harder and smarter because they will be more successful and their work will become more meaningful.

AUTHORITATIVE POWER VS. RELATIONAL POWER

As the result of faltering revenues, the Lebanon school board voted to contract out the cleaning of our school buildings to cut costs and improve services. It was a controversial move. District custodians ended up losing their jobs and a state run rehabilitation firm won the contract for the cleaning. In order to provide some daytime support for maintenance and cleaning during the school day, the district hired facility operators that worked during the school day to provide much needed maintenance in the buildings. Since the positions were new, it was a bit unclear at the beginning what the roles of these new facility operators were exactly.

They received the message from the district office that they were not custodians and shouldn't be involved in custodial duties. At the same time, principals in the buildings expected some kind of custodial/cleaning activities to occur during the school day while they were on duty. Within a week, principals were having conflicts with the facility operators about their job duties. Dr. Hess's school was starting in less than a week, and the contracted cleaners missed a few spots. They had already moved on to other schools and made it clear that they wouldn't be back before the kids arrived.

When Dr. Hess mentioned to the facility operator that the bathrooms needed to be touched up, the trash dumped, and some vacuuming needed to be done, he was shocked to hear the facility operator reply back, "I'm not a custodian." Needless to say, Dr. Hess didn't operate from a position of shared leadership in his response. He informed the facility operator that he would be talking to the district office about his unwillingness to do what was needed to be done. The result of the conversation was a wedge in the relationship rather than a bridge.

Instead of using Dr. Hess's position of authority to cause the facility operator (FO) to submit to his will, he should have employed techniques of shared leadership that would encourage the FO to feel a stronger commitment to the building and the kids. After contemplating this, Dr. Hess realized that to help the FO develop shared leadership for the building he would need to apologize and then discuss ways to help the facility operator avoid custodial obligations while at the same time keep the building clean during special times. In addition, discussion needed to occur so that the contracted folks could be held accountable for the work they needed to do as well.

Managers can win battles and get things done by using their positional power with subordinates, and they might even get faster results in the short run, but leaders cannot develop intrinsic motivation in their employees through positional power. Relational power through shared leadership is the only way to develop intrinsic motivation. Shared leadership takes more time to develop initially, but once someone becomes invested, their involvement in the vision of the organization increases. They become an asset to everything the organization is trying to accomplish. Long-range systemic change and improvement can only be accomplished when co-workers and managers become allies through shared leadership.

EMPOWERMENT RESULTS IN SHARED LEADERSHIP

Empowering others is a key element of shared leadership. Maxwell states, "When a leader can't or won't empower others, that leader creates barriers within the organization that people cannot overcome. If the barriers remain long enough, then the people give up, or they move to another organization where they can maximize their potential" (1998, p. 126). As a leader, you don't get credit for being right. Leadership success is measured by actually taking people where they need to go.

"Leaders are constantly communicating. Leaders communicate more than other people in a group. There is a qualification: most of the time their communication is unconscious and unintentional" (De Pree 1997, p. 70), and the message leaders communicate is either one of shared leadership or controlling management.

Leaders who deliberately and intentionally look for ways to share leadership wind up with empowered individuals around them who are willing to step up, learn new things, and take on new challenges. Leaders who insist on their own way will find themselves increasingly isolated, out of touch, and simply managing from one crisis to the next. If a leader is managing from crisis to crisis, it is a clear indication they are not moving in the realm of shared leadership. Proof of shared leadership is found in the followers (Maxwell 1998).

De Pree (1997) states that potential is wrapped up in the ability of leaders to constantly restore or reweave. The image is of first century fishermen constantly reweaving or restoring their nets so they can catch more fish. The potential for fish is wrapped up in the reweaving or restoration of the net. Effective agents of change are constantly looking at their organizations and people to see what needs to be restored, and they realize that everything is connected. A net held by ten people will catch more fish than the same net held by five, and the work won't be as difficult. People, like nets, wear down, and when we don't invest time in reweaving, potential is lost, and the result of lost potential is isolation, frustration, and crisis management.

The potential of the whole is almost never achieved without regard to the potential of the individual (De Pree 1997). This is one of the reasons why Deming's (1986) model for quality improvement emphasized training so heavily. Highly trained individuals have a greater chance of reaching their potential. Most people do not even approach their potential for a variety of reasons: lack of training, fear of taking risks, and fear of change are just a few. Shared leadership is one of the key ways of unleashing hidden potential. If followers own the inputs, they are more likely to be responsible for the outcomes.

Organizations that approach their potential do so through shared leadership. The whole is greater than the sum of the parts. Extremely talented individuals will only take a team so far. No one argues that the Los Angeles Lakers had the best talent in the 2004 NBA Finals. Led by

Kobe Bryant and Shaquille O'Neal, no one gave the Detroit Pistons a chance. The outcome, however, was much different than expected. Not only did the Pistons win the series, but they did so in decisive fashion, taking the series four games to one—and only one of those games was even close. Their victory was assured because they played as a team with all of the Pistons in-sync, each playing their part. They operated as a high-functioning system sharing the leadership and outmatched the disjointed, more talented group from Los Angeles.

HIRE FOR TALENT

In his classic book *First, Break all the Rules*, Buckingham and Coffman (1999) write about the knowledge, skills, and talents of employees. You can train for knowledge (things to know) and skills (tasks to perform), but you cannot train for talent. Talent can only be refined. Talents are innate qualities unique to each individual. Talent is the oil that makes your knowledge and skills effective. It is talent that makes the difference between good and great. It is talent that makes someone successful. Talent includes all of the intangibles that cannot be measured, such as perseverance, determination, and the ability to relate to others.

In interviewing more than 85,000 managers and supervisors Buckingham and Coffman (1999) discovered that the most successful ones trained effectively for knowledge and skills, but not for talent. The most effective leaders realized that you cannot "put in" talent, you can only draw out what is already there. In other words, you must hire for talent, and past success is the best measurement for the talented.

One of the best examples of hiring for talent in recent years is outlined in the book *Moneyball* (Lewis 2003) which documents how Billy Beane, the manager for the Oakland Athletics, single-handedly changed baseball scouting forever. Prior to Beane's unique approach, baseball scouts looked primarily for skills, or "tools." Could the prospect run, field, hit, and throw? Billy Beane changed all that by harnessing the power of the Internet and analyzing how a potential player actually performed over time. As a result, he discovered a lot of successful players that other scouts overlooked because they were focusing on skills while Billy was looking for talent. A highly skilled individual has potential to perform. A talented individual may possess fewer skills, but they have already demonstrated success. Billy knew intuitively the secret truth others missed—highly skilled individuals are frequently less successful than the talented. Knowledge and skills are important pieces in the process, but talent is the best measure of successful outcomes.

What about the search for hidden talent? What about those who have not yet achieved success, but whose talents are waiting to be discovered? How do you unlock the talent not yet discovered? How do you hire for potential, and is there a way to spot talent in the field of education? There really isn't a set of interview questions that mine for talent. Letters of recommendation do not reveal it. Checking references doesn't quite hit the mark either, and since talent is such an intangible, the best judge of talent is still success over time.

Think of the most successful teachers. What do you notice about them? We define success in teaching as the ability to build positive relationships with students and parents—relationships so positive students become engaged in the curriculum, parents trust the teacher, and high levels of learning are the by-product.

Trust in education these days is not given. It is earned. People do not trust others easily in the twenty-first century, but talented teachers are able to secure it with both their students and parents. Though we can identify the element of positive relationships as the cornerstone to talented teachers, we have also noticed that no two talented teachers build that trust in the same way.

Some talented teachers build trust with parents by regular and frequent phone calls home. Others build it by developing a variety of educational experiences that students enjoy doing. Some teachers are demanding and hard on their students, and the students come to love and appreciate high levels of accountability and the success that comes with it. Other teachers are down-to-earth, friendly, and personal. Some teachers build trust through their outstanding organizational skills, and others through their creativity, innovation, or use of technology in the classroom. Some of the most talented have an expertise or specialty that is engaging because of their deep passion for the material. The list goes on and on. It doesn't take too much reflection to realize that there is no *one way* to be a talented teacher. The process is as varied as the number of talented teachers, but though the process is widely different, the outcome of positive relationships that result in student learning is always the same. For that reason, priority leaders focus on outcomes, not process.

CONTROL THE OUTCOMES, NOT THE PROCESS

Shared leadership does not focus on the process. Shared leadership points a laser-like focus on the desired outcomes and lets the workers choose how to reach those outcomes. In education that means schools and districts need to decide what the outcomes will be. Whether it is grades, proficiency levels on work samples, test scores, attendance rates, or other measurable outcomes, school leaders need to determine what the target will be for student success. Once that target is determined, ways to measure progress must be identified, and then school leaders can get started.

The Signature School movement in Lebanon was a direct result of this philosophy. We defined a signature school as innovative, inviting, and high achieving. Administrative standards were written for each key component. The standards laid out clear expectations of what it meant to be a signature school. Then we turned the schools loose. Schools had the authority and responsibility to take whatever path would most efficiently lead to the achievement of the standards. Research-based best practices were encouraged but not required. Where no research existed, schools were encouraged to develop their own research. No set of instructions was provided from on high explaining how to make it happen.

Controlling management mandates specific curricula and assigned textbooks. Obedient teachers (and frustrated talented ones) follow the program because that is the only materials they have. They follow a predetermined process that the "experts" say is best. The problem is that most experts are trying to sell you something, and nowadays you'll find a lot of experts and professors of "research-based best practices" with conflicting messages. Guess what? They are all right. There is no one "best way" to climb the mountain. The only thing that matters is whether you made it to the top, and how long it took you to get there.

When achievement becomes the constant and time the variable, the only thing that matters is progress toward the standard. It is the outcome that is important, not the process. At Dr. Hess's school, teachers were encouraged *not to use* the district-purchased textbook. They were encouraged to be the teacher—to develop their own curriculum based upon their skills, knowledge, and individual talents. They were given the tools and resources they needed to do their best work. Little attention was paid to process. District requirements became suggestions rather than mandates, and that kind of resistance was *supported* rather than resisted by district leadership because they understood that shared leadership would only occur when the means to achieve the standards was given over completely to teachers and principals.

In the new model, the outcome (progress toward the standards) becomes the all-consuming focus. Given the freedom to innovate, teachers will come alive. They will develop a wide range of systems and ways to advance students toward the standards. When given the permission to leave the textbooks on the shelf, the reality of differentiation emerges, and test scores will go through the roof, but even more importantly, school will become more enjoyable for students because teachers will be more invested in the process. They will own it.

TOP-DOWN AND BOTTOM-UP

In this age of team-building and collaboration it has become anathema to direct decisions from the top of the chain of command to subordinates without having consulted them first. Leaders are encouraged to develop grass roots changes for the value of the "buy-in" or ownership on the part of the members of the organization. Top-down leadership has a negative connotation whereas bottom-up is positive, but the fact is both philosophies are necessary and important depending upon the needs of the situation.

The driving principle in the manner of decision-making should be "as much top-down as necessary and as much bottom-up as possible." Even so, both the bottom and the top must overreach so that a "safety zone" is created in the working relationships such that grass roots efforts are validated and top-down decisions are appreciated and trusted. If people credit "top-down" to the relentless pursuit of a clear and accepted vision, then decisions will not offend. In this safe place, risk taking is possible. It is best described as a place of mutual respect and trust where every member of the group recognizes the responsibility to honor both methods of decision-making.

Controlling managers spend a great deal of time issuing "top-down" decisions. They are constantly micromanaging, dictating curriculum, and other decisions that are best made by the people who are closest to the work being done. They dictate process, firmly believing that following a prescribed path will generate the best results. On the other hand, leaders who do not engage systemic change rely primarily on "bottom-up" decisions and are ineffective as a result. They do not want to generate tension by introducing ideas that may be unpopular.

Supervisors who engage in shared leadership realize that meaningful, systemic change will not happen without movement away from the status quo, and that is not easy, but by providing a safety zone—a place where staff realizes there will be some mandates from management and other decisions they can champion and pursue—continuous progress toward meaningful outcomes is encouraged.

THE JOIN-UP CONCEPT

Monty Roberts, the original "horse whisperer," developed a technique he called "Join-Up" to describe his work with horses over an entire lifetime. The concept revolves around the notion of training horses via collaboration and cooperation rather than compliance. In Monty's system horses are trained to willingly cooperate with the trainer rather than be forced to submit through the age old techniques of pain and intimidation. Monty has demonstrated these techniques in a variety of settings all over the world, and his work was recently portrayed in the film *Horse Whisperer* (1998) starring Robert Redford.

Monty also believed the principles of Join-Up could be applied to the workplace. In *Horse Sense for People* (Roberts 2001), he demonstrates how leaders can create environments where employees want to come to work and give their best effort day after day through cooperation, commitment, and collaboration. The essential idea behind human-to-human Join-Up is for workers to willingly choose to "join-up" with the purposes and priorities of the organization. It is essentially the difference between compliance and commitment in the workplace.

When supervisors operate as controlling managers, they are seeking compliance. Workers are viewed with mistrust and must be kept under control and observation at all times. They are expendable parts of a machine, easily replaced when they break or don't work properly. Most of the time in the world of work, leaders get what they ask for. Leaders that operate as controlling managers get compliance. They also get teachers who check out at 3:00 p.m. each day when the kids leave, live for summer vacation, and do not pursue any learning or training on their own. They will comply. They will follow the rules, and principals will end up with a disinterested, demotivated, disengaged teaching staff who have little value for student learning and whose jobs are protected by powerful unions.

However, when supervisors operate as shared leaders, they understand a fundamental difference about the world of schools. The school environment is more like a system than a machine. In a system—like the solar system, a weather system, or the human body—everything is connected. One part affects the whole, and the pieces cannot be replaced without affecting the entire system. Systems are complex and unpredictable. They do have patterns, but they cannot be controlled. They can only be influenced.

Machines stop and start. They can be turned off and on. They can be controlled. Worn out parts get discarded. New ones replace them, and the machine keeps working. Teachers are not machines. Students are not machines. There is nothing mechanistic about teaching and learning. Shared leaders understand this basic concept, and for this reason, they naturally resist becoming a controlling manager.

The goal of controlled management is compliance. The goal of shared leadership is commitment. Compliance is the result of fear and punishment. It is completely extrinsic. Commitment is internal. The concepts of shared leadership breed commitment. Commitment will not occur without removing fear and intimidation. In schools where there are high levels of commitment, teachers are dedicated to meeting the needs of their students, and they will do whatever it takes to meet those needs. They willingly work in teams, share resources and curriculum with each other, attend conferences, and pursue their own learning on their own time. They'll look for ways to differentiate their curriculum and use effective small group instruction so that they can meet the wide range of learning needs in their classroom. They will share their expertise with others and come to work each day with a smile on their face and leave each afternoon knowing they made a difference. They develop positive relationships with their students, parents, and co-workers. In one word, they are talented. The easiest way for a superintendent to see whether there is a controlling manager or a sharing leader running the building is to look at the environment he or she has created. They will be vastly different and easily distinguished.

SHARED LEADERSHIP DRAWS OUT UNTAPPED POTENTIAL

Very few people have ever reached the limits of their potential. Most of us exist in that comfortable state of what we *think* we can do based upon our experiences, opportunities, and beliefs. If there is no one pouring in encouragement, chances are we perform at a level that is much less than our potential.

The movie *Gatacca* (1997) is about a future society where a person's lifestyle, occupation, and future are all determined by the potential latent within their DNA at birth. Vincent, the young hero of the movie is able to exceed his potential through determination and sheer will power. He never lets go of his dreams. It can be argued that no one exceeds their potential, so when it happens, perhaps we misjudged what they were capable of doing—that is usually the case. Most of us have never dug deep enough to tap our potential or developed our innate talents to full maturation.

Not too long ago, it was a common misconception in the world of public schools that student populations with high numbers of minorities or high levels of poverty would naturally do worse on tests. Educators, reformers, and researchers have been beating that drum for a long time, and mostly it serves as an excuse to not put in the effort, energy, and expertise it will take to help those who come to school with less social capital succeed. Simply because a few decades of test score results show that poor, minority inner-city schools have historically done worse on standardized tests, doesn't mean that students from those backgrounds *aren't capable* of doing better. Being poor doesn't make you stupid. A new interpretation of the data is emerging. Being poor gives you less opportunities and experiences. Having less opportunities limits your potential to perform on standardized tests.

Over the last few years, a number of schools in poor environments are breaking the mold and changing the assumption. Research done by

Douglas Reeves (2004), Robert Barr and William Parrett (2003), Mike Schmoker (1996), and the work of Loraine Monroe at the Harlem Academy demonstrate again and again that students from poverty backgrounds can achieve at high levels—even on standardized tests. These examples of breakthrough results are changing how people interpret data, and showing again and again the importance and power of quality instruction. Latent potential is being unlocked, and that discovery opens up a door of opportunity that was previously closed.

CONCLUSION: MOVING FROM CONTROLLING MANAGEMENT TO SHARED LEADERSHIP

It has often been said that superintendents of schools only have two duties, delegate and supervise. In many ways there is more truth than humor in that statement. Sharing the leadership and letting others lead when they are able is critical to the success of school systems.

Job titles have far less influence than the power of the relationships within a school district. When the relationships are strong and positive good things happen. When they are not, leaders usually resort to their position power to get things done. It would be better advised to work on the relationships; greater things will result.

When talented people are working together the chemistry creates higher expectations, a greater willingness to sacrifice personally for the good of the team, and enhanced outcomes for the system. Leaders must balance their efforts with just enough top-down direction to meet bottom-up grass roots reform at a comfortable place where trust levels secure growth for the system. This is most easily accomplished when leaders focus on the outcomes and allow the followers to determine the process by which the outcomes will be gained.

It is possible to distinguish between leaders and managers by the methods they employ when directing their districts or schools. When superintendents and principals control the process by which things will get done, they are managing. When they set their focus on the outcomes and liberate the workers to determine the means by which to get there, they are leading. Commitment is gained by sharing the leadership. Let it happen and expect the right results.

7

FROM HIDDEN AGENDAS
TO AUTHENTIC LISTENING

Most leaders die with their mouths open. Leaders must know how to
listen—and the art of listening is more subtle than people think it is.

William Taylor

Leaders who arrive with an agenda, or develop one without authentic
listening, inhibit change and improvement. We all know the tricks to
demonstrate you are listening: eye contact, body language, rephrasing,
asking clarifying questions, and so on. Authentic listening is far beyond
what is taught in a freshman psychology class. Authentic listening involves actually putting yourself in the other person's shoes—to experience work and life as they are experiencing it to the greatest degree possible. It takes more than a little imagination to authentically listen. It
also takes a heart to feel what the other person is feeling. Authentic listening protects us from having an agenda and frees us to pursue innovation and growth through effective change.

In his research, Collins discovered that one of the consistent characteristics of companies that transformed from good to great was what he
termed their "relationship to the window and the mirror" (Collins 2001,
p. 33). When the great companies became successful, the chief leaders
attributed their success to those outside the window, the people in the

company who worked hard to make it successful. When struggles arose, these same leaders looked in the mirror to determine what they were doing wrong, and how they could change in order to turn things around. By contrast, the companies that never became great had leaders who consistently pointed to the workers when there were problems and patted themselves on the back when things went well. In the world of sports, great coaches operate in the same manner. They credit the team in seasons of victory and look to themselves for how to improve in times of defeat.

FIND THE EXPERTS AND DO NOT BLAME

Blaming others is a hindrance to authentic listening. When leaders' egos get in the way, it is not possible for them to find out what is really going on in the field. Their egos will filter them from understanding the facts, and they will constantly be missing cues that they are in trouble. Authentic listening begins by removing all filters to the data, and that can only be done through careful observation and soliciting the input of a variety of individuals and data sources. Reeves (2005) talks about the importance of multiple data points in order to get a true assessment of how a school or district is progressing to make accountability meaningful. Change agents with agendas end up pushing *their plans* and the result is a lack of buy-in and commitment from those around them. Authentic listening involves taking the time to feel the heartbeat of the organization, and no two heartbeats are alike.

The most effective and best known leaders in the airline business: Jan Carlzon with Scandinavian Airlines System (SAS) in the early 1980s, Colin Marshall at British Airways in the 1990s, and Herb Kelleher at Southwest Airlines were known for flying on their own airlines. They were always talking to customers and encouraging ticket agents and baggage handlers to creatively solve problems. They were in the "dynamic listening" mode, asking questions all the time—not being tempted to provide all the answers (Taylor 1999). They knew intuitively that it was the employees closest to work who had the best solutions. These outstanding, unusual leaders listened to their own experts and learned how to improve their business.

SONAR AS A METAPHOR FOR AUTHENTIC LISTENING

Many times we engage in conversations with the notion that we are listening with undivided attention. The truth of the matter, however, is that we are constructing responses as we process the speech of the other person, and we end up making faulty assumptions about the message the other person is trying to convey. We begin to frame our response not only from what we've heard but also what we've necessarily assumed about the meaning as well. When it is a simple conversation between two people, any misperceptions can be easily corrected before moving the conversation along. It is another matter when leaders need to hear their followers.

Leaders have agendas, priorities, goals, and expectations that orient them to the tasks that move their organizations forward. When we allow these things to predominate over the collective voice of our followers, we are guilty of agenda building. We often spend more time persuading others of the merits of our chosen course then we do in reading their concerns or criticisms where constructive revisions can enable greater progress. The consequence of this behavior is to stilt the organization and to create a system that is out of balance with itself. People know the agenda but are uncomfortable with the manner in which it is being pursued. Followers do not feel "listened to." Alternatively, members of an organization do not know the motives for the agenda and believe that something is hidden from them. Trust begins to erode. Administration is accused of a hidden agenda, and in the words of Steve Robbins (2005), "Trust can be gained once and lost once. Once lost, it's lost forever."

In reality, there is probably nothing hidden, but the sales pitch is intense enough that a sense of disempowerment settles in on the organization. People feel somewhat disenfranchised and seek to lay blame for their feelings. It is a delicate balance that leaders must strike to afford people a chance to feedback information about their levels of "buy-in" without feeling like they've sacrificed the mission or agenda that they are encouraging. Nevertheless, it is absolutely necessary to gain a sense of employee perspective to navigate through these treacherous moments.

Like ships at sea, it is difficult to navigate if you can't see where you are going. It might also be compared to flying blind. Pilots trust their instrumentation to direct them safely where they would otherwise surely fail. Radar and sonar have become critical to the success of pilots of sea and air.

The art of authentic listening is the leader's sonar or radar. Sound navigation ranging is the detection and location of underwater objects by means of reflecting acoustic waves from these objects. The result is the avoidance of disaster and the safe navigation of the ship. If we listen with the same purpose in mind we can pilot our organizational ship through stormy seas and hidden obstacles to safe harbor as well. Radar uses similar principles with electromagnetic waves. When it comes to using listening in our leadership, the first question now surfaces: How do we develop our sonar or radar to help us navigate our course?

We must begin by turning it on. When we control the agenda and try to drive the organization in the direction we think it should go, we often do so without regard for the obstacles that lie before us. In the physical world it is easier to recognize the hazards. When we can't see them, we grow even more cautious because we know that they are out there somewhere. In the world of leadership we fail to appreciate the obstacles that are surely before us. We move straight ahead with great dispatch mindless to the perils of such reckless pursuits. We do need to be action-oriented, but only so far as we are equipped to recognize the dangers in our pathway. When ships are operating in shallow waters, they slow and proceed with caution. They trust their sonar to identify the shoals and reefs that create graveyards full of hulls.

In order to avoid the hidden dangers, we must give the responses to our signals undivided attention. We cannot be thinking about the next question nor assume that we understand where a particular response is headed. We cannot seek to "win the argument." It would also be foolhardy to think that we already know the way because we've sailed the waters before. Even if the questioning produces anticipated results, we have then affirmed our course of action. Accuracy in the hearing is critical to the successful navigation of any leader-ship. Any distractions can be perilous. As the pilot of the leader-ship, you must listen with the intent to take diversionary or evasive action. Be ready to redirect your pathway. Listen with the intent to be changed.

The second question is equally important. What do we use to send out the signal that will bounce back to us for our readings? Questions act as the sonar to help us find the best course to take. We should be constantly questioning with the full intent of reading the responses to take diversionary or evasive action when necessary. Do not assume nor argue with the message you receive. Trust the instrumentation. If it is faulty, it should not be presumed in the response but in the signal—the question that was asked. Leaders must ask the right questions to get accurate readings that will direct the way. Faulty questions create faulty responses and thus our gauges present a picture that is inaccurate.

We navigate our pathway by active and authentic listening. Authentic listening, like sonar, is listening with the intent to create movement. Sonar sends out a signal and waits for a response, so that the system can *act* upon that response. Authentic listening—like the effective use of sonar—causes movement. It is a generator of change. Organizations that learn and grow are directed by authentically listening to the voices of the people involved.

OPEN SPACE AS A TOOL FOR AUTHENTIC LISTENING

Management consultant Harrison Owen developed Open Space Technology (OST) in 1983. It grew out of his frustration with conventional conferences that required hours of preplanning and preparation that left participants wanting something more. He observed that the coffee break conversations were more powerful than the conversations that occurred in the planned sessions, thus illustrating the classic struggle of external versus internal control. Only we can determine what is meaningful for us. External stimuli such as lectures, displays, speakers, and panel discussions are hit and miss. In most cases these are one-way interactions that deliver more stuff—remember the traditional classroom—then determine what people need and deliver the staff development accordingly. Sitting and getting is hardly the type of activity that will build capacity. In most cases, the participant attends these conferences in search of the answers. They want the presenters to solve their problems in 90 minutes or less. When this does not happen, the participants leave frustrated at the conference organizers and/or the presenters for their inability to meet their needs. The cycle continues. Harrison Owen sought a way to break this cycle by sharing ownership for growth with both the *learner* and the presenter. OST can be used by leaders to help surface hidden issues and move beyond hidden agendas. It can be the first step in pursuing the priority of authentic listening.

BEING RESPONSIBLE FOR YOUR LEARNING

OST is predicated on people taking responsibility for their actions. It is a facilitative structure that allows large groups of people to think collaboratively around complex issues that they are most passionate about. Passion and responsibility are the key values in any OST event. OST provides the structure to build on passion and responsibility.

Open space is best used with complex issues that need a number of people to tackle the problem. It responds to leadership opportunities and seeks to help people connect and resolve issues that go to the heart of their professional experience. If the problem is the revamping of the school's recess schedule (a management dilemma) then OST is not the right tool.

An OST gathering begins by organizing around a theme. The theme should be compelling enough to draw out the passion of those who are affected by the very questions that are presented. It is the means to authentically listen to the needs and dilemmas of the people. The invited group must be interested and committed. OST events should always be voluntary. In order to capture people's true passions and responsibilities—to authentically listen—they must come to the event willingly. People will usually have the final say about what is important to them. OST provides the opportunity for the leaders to "practice what they preach" and really listen to the needs and hearts of the people immersed in the struggle. Diverse perspectives are another important factor in the OST group. Such diversity of thought breeds new ideas and new ideas lead to innovation. Effective OST groups bring people from a variety of perspectives.

To make an OST event successful, the physical setting must be conducive to having multiple conversations that will take place simultaneously. A large meeting room for the initial and closing ceremonies is required with several breakout rooms for the mini-sessions that will follow. A large wall that will hold the community news as well as the group-created agenda is also a necessity. The OST event must be run without interruption. Participants should not drop in and out. Breaks and lunch should be served on site so as not to interrupt the flow of conversation that will exist as long as the "open space" is left open.

Most OST events last from one to three days. The number of participants can range from 20 to 400-plus. It is ideal for very large groups. The opening ceremony is usually conducted in one or two concentric circles. An informal opening usually works best, especially for intact groups. Formal icebreaking activities are not used. The OST facilitator explains the basic structure and processes of OST. At this time the facilitator stresses the values of passion and responsibility and the *law of two feet*.

THE LAW OF TWO FEET

The law of two feet is extremely simple but outstandingly powerful. It is an application of responsibility. If a person finds oneself in a conversation that is not producing any learning for that individual or contributing to the learning of others, then that person must move to another conversation that will provide those results. In other words, the individuals are responsible for their learning, not the presenters or the OST facilitator. Most people struggle with this law in the beginning. The OST facilitator must stress its importance.

If orchestrated properly, OST mines the depths of the participants' intents and hearts. No one will leave the event without learning about some issue that is important to them because they are in charge, not the people around them. This is a new experience for most people who are products of traditional American classrooms. It would be rude for someone to leave in the middle of a class or presentation. In OST, it is required.

After explaining the OST values and laws, the group begins to build the agenda. Normally an agenda would be set prior to the conference by the conference organizer. In building the agenda for OST, each participant may come to the center of the circle and declare their topic of conversation. They write it on chart paper and attach it to the agenda wall for further discussion. Such discussion takes place after all participants have had a chance to "convene" a session on a topic that they will take responsibility for and have real passion about. It is an explosive combination. After all topics have been posted on the wall, the group will take some time to negotiate the time and places of all these sessions. It is common to have very large groups take only 30–45 minutes to accomplish this enormous task. It is critical to the success of OST for this type of agenda building to take place. Once the agenda is built and posted on the wall, all participants are invited to come forth and declare which sessions they will attend. This will assist in room assignment based on the number of requested participants. There may also be conflict or combinations of sessions that may occur. It is important that any modification of sessions be done with consent of the conveners.

Conveners are responsible for facilitating the conversations in their sessions as well as any pertinent information that is generated by the discussion groups. All session notes are captured and copies are given to all participants at the end of the conference. The meeting minutes can be posted on a community bulletin board for all participants to see. At the end of each day there is an evening news or closing session, depending on the length of the conference. The closing session is simple but serious. People are given an opportunity to reflect on the sessions they have attended. Not everyone will be asked to respond. It should be a voluntary activity. In most cases, people will talk about the passion they have experienced during the event as well as the responsibility for some type of action that will follow the conference. It's important to celebrate the closing. Particularly in multi-day events, a celebration at the end will honor everyone's hard work and value the time and energy that they have committed to the process.

The priority leader understands the importance of open agendas and uses OST tools and philosophies throughout the organization in order to authentically listen to the people and act upon the collective knowledge and wisdom of the group. It is not necessary to wait for the annual conference to use OST ideas. It does not have to be a special event to create "Open Space."

What would happen if leaders made all staff meetings voluntary or allowed people to use the law of two feet in these meetings? Would people stop coming? Or would only the people who truly cared about making a difference get involved? Allowing staff members to create the agenda by submitting items during the time prior to the meeting is one way of using OST to authentically listen. Staff would also be responsible for conducting the discussion when that item comes up on the agenda. Staff development days would look much different if we used OST techniques. Rather than the traditional "stand and deliver" or the "expert presenter" models, staff development days could be organized around volunteer staff members—teacher leaders—convening sessions for their fellow staff members who would sign up for their session. With the use of the law of two feet, staff members could attend multiple sessions according to their interest and level of participation, which will drive higher levels of learning and application of knowledge.

THE POWER OF CRITICAL FRIENDS TO EXPEDITE AUTHENTIC LISTENING

The critical friends movement has gained momentum in recent years as a powerful reflective activity that helps educators discover solutions to difficult problems through the power of authentic listening. The Critical Friends Group (CFG) training is extensive. Through the training, facilitators learn a variety of protocols that enable them to help groups of educators share and discover solutions to complex issues and needy situations. The goal of CFGs is to build "the trust needed to engage in direct, honest, and productive conversations with colleagues about the complex art of teaching (Bambino 2002, p. 25). CFGs can be formed around analyzing student work, applying professional growth standards to instruction, or trying to discover a course of action for a multifaceted dilemma.

In Lebanon, we were able to develop university partnerships through federal improvement grants to provide CFG training and facilitate their start up and development. When CFGs function properly, they are powerful vehicles to help educators hear and be heard by their peers in a safe environment where reflection, shared accountability, and feedback can occur without the stigma of failure (Lindstrom and Speck 2004). In many ways, CFGs are a formal tool for helping an organization's members listen authentically to each other.

TRANSFORMING CHANGE: BUILDING TRUST TO LEAD

Transforming, systemic change is a by-product of an environment that has high levels of trust built through authentic listening. An administrator's time is divided into two basic types of activities: leadership and management. Simply put, you manage things and lead people. People respond to leadership with integrity and trust. Effective leaders earn that trust on a daily basis through their activities. The four C's of competence, commitment, caring and courage are effective ways to build trust through authentic listening.

Competence

Competence is step one for the priority leader. Administrators cannot lead if they cannot manage. They must be competent. The trains must run on time. Phone calls need to be returned, e-mails answered, and paperwork turned in. The day-to-day operation of the building or district must run smoothly. Budgets, communications, schedules, and agendas must meet the orderly expectations of all stakeholders. More importantly, the administrator should be knowledgeable in all areas of education. He or she must be competent in the areas of managerial administration.

Commitment

Everyone watches the leader. They look for weaknesses. They look for strengths. They look to see how the leader spends time and adjusts their behavior accordingly. It doesn't take long for staff members to understand the commitment level of their leader. Commitment is not determined by time spent as much as by how leaders *spend their time.* Everyone is committed to something. Priority leaders are committed to the right things. They are committed to building relationships through conversation, through authentic listening. They are committed to continuous improvement. They are committed to the rejection of the status quo. They are committed to the growth of every staff member, and helping each one achieve their true, and sometimes hidden, potential. Being committed to the right things fosters an environment of support and caring.

Caring

We've all heard the old adage, "People don't care how much you know until they know how much you care." Just because it's trite doesn't mean it isn't true. It is a mistake for change-oriented leaders to be so committed to the business that staff do not feel valued or supported. It may save time and energy in the short run to scrimp on caring, but in the big picture, employees who do not feel supported will develop an "eight to four" attitude. Teaching is a stressful profession. Teachers are underpaid for their effort and work. Society does not value them like they used to. In the current climate of accountability, there is more pressure put on teachers than ever before. Each and every year they are working under more and more stressful conditions of increased class size, test score improvement, student difficulty, and parent demands. If they don't feel valued as a person by their leader, it doesn't take the average teacher long to learn to begin to cut corners, and the extra effort it takes to meet student needs doesn't occur. Priority leaders place a high value on caring and make time to demonstrate they care for those they lead.

People don't always have to agree on the issues or the outcomes of those issues but everyone wants to be valued. Everyone wants to be heard. To make a connection, to create community, a leader must listen to every conversation with the *intent to be changed* by the conversation. Listening with the intent to be changed dissolves hidden agendas. It is the key to authentic listening, and it is the best way to genuinely care for those with whom you work. We are convinced that if all leaders could listen in this fashion our abilities to create meaningful, engaging communities would grow exponentially. Listening with the intent to be changed does not mean that we easily alter our core values and ideas, or do we tell people what they want to hear after we have "listened to them." But it does mean that we genuinely care about what people think and how they feel, and since we care, we enter every conversation listening with the intent or potential to be changed—to learn and grow through the conversation.

Courage

Courage is the necessary fourth ingredient for authentic listening to occur. It takes courage to re-examine your beliefs. It takes courage to help others explore their core values and beliefs. It takes courage to change, and when people are willing to change, they need to be recognized for their courage. It takes courage to tell the truth. Truth telling is necessary for real trust and listening to occur. Authentic connections between people allow leaders to have honest conversations that will systemically move organization toward change. When high levels of trust have been established through authentic listening, the transforming change conversations will occur.

CONCLUSION: MOVING FROM HIDDEN AGENDAS TO AUTHENTIC LISTENING

Authentic listening is a vehicle of reflection that allows an individual or organization to see themselves as they truly are rather than what they hope or think they are. The key purpose of authentic listening is to not only expose your true self, but to act upon that knowledge. Priority leaders check their hidden agendas at the door. They truly engage in collaboration and reflection with the intent to uncover the truth in an environment of trust and respect and act upon that knowledge so that greater improvement can be achieved.

8

FROM CONFORMANCE TO PERFORMANCE

The signs of outstanding leadership appear primarily among the followers. Are the followers reaching their potential? Are they learning? Serving? Do they achieve the required results? Do they change with grace? Manage conflict?

Max De Pree

The pressure to conform is a great hindrance to improvement, innovation, and increased performance. Conforming results in mediocrity. Continuous improvement is the benchmark of excellence and is marked by one solid performance after another. Leaders in their fields are not conformists. They are not waiting for someone to tell them what to do. They have ideas—lots of them—and they continually bring them forward in an effort to break the status quo to increase performance.

At Booker T. Washington High School in Memphis, Tennessee, principal Elsie Lewis Bailey has increased teacher leadership by turning over to her staff the task of designing the school schedule and activities. In the fall each teacher joins a planning group that looks at one aspect of the school. As a result of one of these study groups, staff suggested that each teacher should advise/mentor five at-risk ninth-graders throughout their high school career. Since teachers suggested the intervention, there was increased buy-in, which is a necessary element of increased results (Krajewski 2005).

At Bret Harte Middle School in Oakland, California, innovative leaders have broken the mold of conformance by developing cross-grade clusters scheduled on a rotating basis (Renzulli et al. 2004). The clusters meet weekly for a double-period block to pursue authentic learning experiences developed around teacher strengths and interests. These enrichment clusters are not mini-courses. There is no predetermined content to cover. Each one investigates a real life problem and seeks solutions. Clusters are designed around political opinions, investigating community recycling needs, researching historical artifacts, creative writing, producing a play, designing an instructional website, designing scenery, improving a landscape, or a hundred other real life challenges that need solutions. This school has discovered the fact that "improved test scores are important, but it's the *application* of knowledge in an authentic learning situation" that truly matters in the long run (Renzulli et al. 2004, p. 74).

Even though most public school districts in America are vigorously pursuing a path of conformity to rigorous grade level testing in order to demonstrate Adequate Yearly Progress (AYP), high performing schools that value quality above all do not succumb to the mandated testing mentality. They seek higher and higher levels of performance and benchmark their success to what they know truly matters: facilitating life-long, authentic learning that is based in performance.

One of the most radical movements of authentic, performance-based learning happening like brush fires across the United States is found in the small high school reform movement called The Big Picture. Chronicled in a book by the same title, *The Big Picture* (Littky 2004), the big picture movement proposes radically changing how the average high school functions. In the big picture, individual student needs and interests take the driver's seat. Big Picture Schools have a student body of around a hundred students. Cohorts of 20 to 25 students are partnered with one advisor who works with the students and their families for 4 years. The advisor becomes closely connected with each student and helps them find and pursue internships where they learn off site two days a week. In these innovative schools, there are no tests and no grades. Students demonstrate their learning through portfolios and exhibitions where they present their findings before peers, parents, and community partners. There are over twenty-five Big Picture Schools across the country and another twenty-five on the launch pad. Big Picture Schools accept a wide range of students—from ones who have already dropped out of traditional high schools to former home school students, to other students just looking for a non-traditional high school experience. These schools are showing remarkable attendance rates and very few behavior problems. Student scores on mandatory state tests are exceeding those of traditional schools. The Big Picture movement is another example that pursuing a quality experience does not diminish the quality of the product.

THE AGONY OF CONFORMANCE: THE ABILENE PARADOX

In 1974, George Washington University Professor Jerry Harvey converted a real life experience into the management insight known as the Abilene Paradox (Harvey 1988). In his parable about organizational dysfunction, Jerry is sitting on a porch in 104-degree heat in the small town of Coleman, Texas, some 53 miles from Abilene with his wife and in-laws. In an attempt to keep from overheating, the family is engaging in as little motion as possible: drinking lemonade, watching the fan spin lazily, and occasionally playing a game of dominoes. In the lull of the afternoon, Jerry's father in-law suggests they drive to Abilene to eat at a diner. Jerry thinks the idea is crazy. It is blistering hot, and the old Buick has no air conditioning, but he doesn't want to voice his disagreement to the suggestion. The two women nod their heads in agreement as well, and the ill-fated trip through the prairie to Abilene is underway.

Over the course of the next several hours, the group eats a mediocre meal at an Abilene diner and returns to Coleman late that afternoon exhausted, hot, and generally unhappy with the whole experience. Back on the porch in Coleman, one after another of the group not only voices his or her displeasure with the trip but the fact they didn't really want to go in the first place. The father-in-law admits he only suggested the trip to be polite. He had no intention of going and was hoping someone would have voiced disagreement to the idea. In the end it turns out they were all going along with the suggestion because they thought the others were eager to go, and no one wanted to step into the uncomfortable world of disagreement. The Abilene Paradox is the ultimate example of conformist behavior: under the pressure to avoid conflict, people have a natural tendency to conform by not sharing their true feelings and thoughts.

The extraordinary question that emerges from the story is, "Why would individuals speak in opposition to their own desires?" Such frequent group behavior stems from fear of the consequences of speaking "their own minds" and their creation of "negative fantasies" about the possible outcomes from speaking their minds. People fear intellectual, emotional, or physical separation from the group to which they belong, and that fear of separation prevents them from speaking their true opinion.

As a result, people imagine the worst and create fantasies that give cause to inaction and actually speak against their own wishes. This level of conformance leads organizations and institutions to underperform and even to fail. Ironically, the consequences of such collusion or tyranny are the very outcomes the misguided conversation sought to avoid—separation from one another. The separation can be ostracism, termination, demotion, or simply a faultfinding argument.

The cycle of wrong assumptions and fear can permeate an organization's culture. New communication skills are required to create more appropriate patterns of behavior that significantly reduce the victimization of all of the members of the group or organization. It is important to remember that everyone inaccurately portrayed the situation by speaking against his or her own beliefs or feelings. As a result, no one is to blame, but in fact all are victims and equally responsible for modifying their communication patterns to become more authentic when communicating their desires, feelings, or beliefs.

Conformance of the sort created by the Abilene Paradox is almost always harmful to the organization and to the individuals who are engaged in it. When healthier means of communication are developed, we move from conformance to higher levels of positive performance. The Abilene Paradox speaks to the importance of *managing agreement* in order to avoid conformance behavior.

MANAGING AGREEMENT

Peter Senge's *The Fifth Discipline Fieldbook* (1994) provides several practices that help groups break the dysfunctional cycle of the misrepresented agreement that threatens them and strategies on how to avoid conformance behavior. Individuals can use the practice of listing "What's Being Said" against "What I Am Thinking." The discrepancies must be addressed in order to avoid the possibility that assumptions are made contrary to the individual's thoughts. In this two-column exercise participants list what the group is saying versus what they are thinking. Environments of trust and mutual support must be created so that individuals are willing to share their individual thoughts without fear of separation from the relationship of the group.

Group members must learn to balance advocacy with inquiry. Genuine inquiry frees people from their biases long enough to explore the possibilities that others may favor. If we are always found advocating for our own positions or remain condescending or silent, we destroy the opportunities we have to manage agreement. The ability to weigh in on our own assumptions is critical to the clarification of beliefs within a group. Chris Argyris' Ladder of Inference (Senge 1994) is an excellent tool because it enables us to analyze our inferences and verify their accuracy. In using the ladder of inference, participants practice dispelling assumptions in order to reveal true feelings and facts.

As individuals develop the art of dialogue, open-ended exploration can replace the tyranny of agreement and conformance that all groups naturally drift toward. Group members must develop the confidence that one is free to speak one's own mind without the threat of ostracism or alienation in order to break the cycle. When trust is present within a group, it is easier to risk disagreement and conflict that might surface when individuals share their true thoughts and feelings.

THE POWER OF CHOICE

Providing choice generates movement toward performance. When people have the opportunity to make choices, they take a greater ownership in their actions and have a tendency to perform better. When teachers have few choices, whether it is over their curriculum, students in their classroom, or work assignment, the drift will be to conformance and underachievement. Whenever possible, choice or preferences, should be considered and honored. In Lebanon, we discovered the value of signature schools to foster innovation and greater performance through preference. Under the signature school priority, each district school was encouraged and supported in their quest to pursue innovations. Naturally, these innovations leaned toward the personal preferences of staff members and their local school community. In many cases, alternative calendars developed complete with intersessions, a variety of after school programs, early releases, and late starts. Though the differing calendars created levels of chaos at times for the district office and transportation, the freedom and support for choice helped move each school toward higher levels of performance and away from conforming behavior.

ACCOUNTABILITY: THE BIG PICTURE

> As educators, we have two choices. We can rail against the system, hoping that standards and testing are a passing fad, or we can lead the way in a fundamental reformulation of educational accountability. We can wait for policymakers to develop holistic accountability plans, or we can be proactive in exceeding the requirements of prevailing accountability systems. (Reeves 2004, p. 6)

Prevailing thought among educators is that accountability measures are not only here to stay, but are going to increase (Johnson 2004). Our choice is not whether we are accountable, but whether we will march to the external accountability drums of policymakers or create our own internal accountability measures to track what we know is truly important in education. If all of our attention is directed to the accountability mandates of others, we will end up conforming to mediocrity and the vision of those outside the system. On the other hand, if we choose to pursue our own internal measures of performance, outside accountability will not be an issue. We will exceed their expectations.

When it comes to accountability, there are the aforementioned measures (see p. 76) that we can look at to judge success: the quality of experience and the quality of product. The quality of product refers to those things that can be easily measured and compared: test score data, attendance rates, reading, writing, and math levels, the number of suspensions and expulsions, the number of teachers with master's degrees, and years of experience.

Quality of experience concerns the intangibles of education that are not as easily measured and compared but are equally important to the success of a school. They include a student's perceptions about schooling; whether they like their teacher; whether they feel safe. Is there someone who will listen to them when they have a problem? Is their something at the school for them, and do they fit in? The quality of experience is harder to measure because the data is mostly qualitative and can only be obtained through interviews, observations, and surveys. In terms of time and money, it is more expensive to collect; nevertheless school district leaders should pursue quality of experience indicators. When it comes to overall student and school success, the quality of experience is as important—perhaps even *more important*—than the quality of product because when it comes to quality, if someone's experience is poor, the chances are greater they will be under-performing on tests or attending school more infrequently. In other words, quality of experience is directly related to the quality of the product.

A recent study of principals indicated that when it comes to quality, principals talk about quality of experience values at a rate of two to one over the quality of product indicators (Hess 2005). If we as educators can help students have a high-quality experience in school, they will be happy, productive, and more likely to perform to their academic potential. An example of what is possible by pursuing quality of experience can be found at the Arts and Technology Public Charter School (ATA) in Washington, D.C.

A 20-minute drive from the White House, ATA is a ray of sunshine in a neglected neighborhood marked by high levels of poverty, crime, housing projects and convenience stores that speak to customers through bulletproof glass (Camelleri and Jackson 2005) The school has only been in existence since 1999 and currently boasts an enrollment of 620 students. The student body is 98.8 percent African American with a free and reduced lunch rate of 95 percent. ATA stands out not only because they have demonstrated test score improvement and increased attendance rates, but even more importantly, they have integrated the arts and technology throughout all of the academic disciplines. Common planning periods enable teachers to help each other prepare and develop lessons in every subject using arts as a teaching tool. A variety of performing arts groups enable students to learn beyond the classroom. The school has an extended day and school year program for struggling students, and they actively recruit and retain quality teachers by rewarding excellent teaching through financial incentives, bonuses, or compensation for taking classes and attending conferences. Through individualized learning plans, ATA has made quality of experience the top priority and considers their work successful if a student leaves the school not only academically prepared but also able "to strive for individual achievement, to cooperate with and be compassionate toward peers, and to approach the surrounding world with curiosity and joy" (Camelleri and Jackson 2005, p. 64).

WHEN QUALITY OF EXPERIENCE IS LACKING

The reverse is true as well. Unfortunately, there have been many acts of violence and school shootings during the last 15 years. Some of these cases are high profile media events, but many more occur under the radar and greatly diminish the quality of our schools. When one analyzes the causes of these acts of violence, it becomes clear that few of them occurred because a student earned low test scores. Case after case is caused because a student was not having a good experience in school. They were being bullied, teased, or felt isolated. Many of those who have resorted to violence were extremely intelligent students who came across as successful on the quality of product measures; they had good test scores. However, if their quality of experience had been measured, they would have surfaced as an at-risk student. Policymakers have been seriously targeting test scores (and now legislating measurable improvement) since uniform state standards were developed in the early 1990s (Hess 2005). It is time to pay serious attention to the quality of a student's experience, and this will not happen from the state or federal level. Local leaders must invest the time and money to measure and improve every student's quality of experience, and as we engage in that noble work, we will see measurable test score improvement as well.

ACCOUNTABILITY AND CONFLICT AS A TENSION GENERATOR

Leaders who effectively initiate change that yields measurable improvement have to be willing to take risks, step out of line, and see if anyone will follow. They are not afraid to generate tension to change the status quo. In order to reach our potential, all organizations and individuals need accountability. Accountability is here to stay. Conflict will always exist. Our choice is how we use accountability and conflict as tension generators for positive results.

There are many ways to introduce tension into a system. One of the most crucial, but often overlooked, is the necessity for tension on the executive team itself. A management team that uses conflict as a tension generator will arrive at the best ideas available and will avoid boarding buses to Abilene. Every system requires tension—or adversity—to grow, change, and become stronger. Comfort, or equilibrium, is the enemy of growth (Pascale et al. 2000).

Many leaders do not want conflict and avoid it like the plague. They want people to be comfortable. Unfortunately, the best ideas will usually only materialize when a sense of disequilibrium is felt. Patrick Lencioni (2002) declares that fear of conflict is a dysfunction that will bury effective teams. He states that conflict is never fun nor easy, and one never gets used to it, but it is necessary for healthy teams to enter into conflict as a regular discipline because it is through conflict that the most effective ideas emerge. When teams are willing to face off and enter into conflict, that is a sign of trust and commitment not only to other team members but to each one's willingness to commit to the team. Learning to engage in healthy conflict is not a one-time event, but an ongoing discipline.

Looking to hire people with diverse backgrounds is another way to generate healthy tension on a leadership team. Management guru Dee Hock was fond of saying:

Never hire or promote in your own image. It is foolish to replicate your strength. It is idiotic to replicate your weakness. It is essential to employ, trust, and reward those whose perspective, ability, and judgment are radically different from yours. It is also rare, for it requires uncommon humility, tolerance, and wisdom. (as cited in Waldrop 1996, p. 79)

Proactively identifying and resolving conflict is a way to strengthen relationships and increase performance. Successfully processing conflict is an often-overlooked chance to build bridges and understanding among team members. Successful businesses like Southwest Airlines invest significant time in conflict resolution (Gittell 2003) and have a protocol for surfacing, owning, and resolving conflict. Gittell goes so far as to say that "organizations should proactively seek out conflicts rather than allow them to fester" (Gittell 2003, p. 113).

Conflict is ever present just as every new day has its weather. Sometimes we don't recognize it or remember it until it storms. Conflict resolution should be understood as a means for processing disagreements, not as a tool to eliminate conflict from the team. Conflict should be a frequent point at which the team effectively processes it for the growth of the organization, and it is through the vehicle of conflict that the best and most stable ideas surface.

CONCLUSION: MOVING FROM CONFORMANCE TO PERFORMANCE

Targeting quality of experience by creating schools and districts that help each student reach not only their academic potential, but their *life* potential will result in breakthrough performance. That's just one way we can move our school districts away from conforming to the mandates of test-happy policymakers. There is a strong research base showing that high expectations have a direct correlation to increased performance (Reeves 2004). The quality of experience is a higher bar than the quality of product. By targeting quality of experience, we are aiming for a higher, nobler, more worthy goal that is better for students and their parents than merely trying to improve test scores. Test scores will follow best practice and excellent teaching because we know that instructional quality is the number one factor for student success (Lieberman and Miller 2004). The key to moving from conformance to performance is relatively simple to identify: discover and implement best practices through highly trained teachers and continually target quality of experience. Identification, however, is just the beginning. Results only follow good ideas if there is action to implement and sustain good ideas over time—including the use of conflict as a tension generator for team commitment and growth.

FROM TRADITION TO DATA TO REFLECTION

Reflection is precisely the capacity to distance oneself from the highly routinized, depleting, sometimes meaningless activities in which we are engaged, so that we can see what's really going on. There is a useful distinction between reflecting *in* practice and reflection *on* practice.

Roland Barth

"That's the way we've always done it."

"That's just the way things are around here."

These and similar comments reflect an organization that has established a dominate tradition which suppresses change and overrides current real life situations. Such occurrences can be positive or negative. The effect is to provide comfort and security through long held norms and ways of behaving within the organization. Ironically, it may also lead to the breakdown of human community. Trusting tradition alone is usually injurious to our working relationships.

Tradition within an organization is a coherent body of time-honored practices and precedents that are influencing the present. If tradition is maintained without proper reflection on the value of long held beliefs, practices, and precedents, an organization becomes trapped in the status quo. Purpose and progress are clouded and restricted. Tradition and culture do have their place within organizations. They simply need to be maintained in ways that make them amenable to modification and renewal. This is achieved when sufficient time is given to the practice of reflection on the merits, benefits, and advantages of the tradition and culture. Moreover, the organization needs to project the needs of the present on the cultural traditions that are still operating.

REFLECTION IS INTERNAL

Organizations on the fast track of growth are filled with individuals who are internally driven to perform. Reflection is a powerful tool for those who are internally motivated. Our experiences and life events are the raw material out of which we derive meaning for the improvement of the organization. Reflection attempts to identify and interpret others' and our experiences in ways that are meaningful for the present set of circumstances facing the organization. Reflection provides the context for individuals to identify and state the guiding principles that ground an institution's priorities.

Reflection must necessarily draw on real life experiences within the organization as well as the traditions of the organization in a correlated way thereby framing the practical implications for the system. This has the effect of putting the reflections of the organization's members into context. Members must share what has happened to them, reflect on the happenings, and then recreate practices and precedents that renew commitments to the institution's priorities. When the tradition and resources of the institution's culture are melded with the experiences of the community and its members, then relevant information is produced directing the pathways to the future of the organization.

More specifically, the reflective conversations within the organization must be personal but also community related. Everyone's voice must be heard. Honest contemplation of the message is required to bring integrity to the process. To engage in reflection is to open an ongoing conversation that includes aspects of the past, present, and future. It is undertaken with the intent of establishing the members' interdependence and a solid community bent on meaningful action.

Reflection is a form of exploration into the corporate and individual experiences of an organization with the knowledge of its history. When we apply our beliefs and perspectives to that exploration we are able to create new ways of working for the good of all concerned. We do not want to be locked into the past, nor do we want to venture into new frontiers without history's lesson. Therefore, we should exercise reflection upon the current purposes and events of the organization and its history with the intent of creating improvement and a renewed corporate spirit.

Reflection is the corporate introspection and examination of the beliefs, practices, history, and purposes of an organization. Schools and organizations have been beating the data drum for a few years now. Reflection is deeper than data. Reflection implies acting upon what the data reveals. It is the careful consideration of where we've been, where we are, and where we're going that is critical to revision, enhancement, and renewal of the system. It takes the commitment of all of the members of the organization to bring their intellects, memories, hopes, and wounds to the analysis of the real life situations that confront them in the present.

REFLECTION IS THE HEART OF EXCELLENT TEACHING

Reflection is one of the most powerful tools for improving teaching performance. Teachers that are meeting student needs are constantly reflecting on what they are doing and how effectively they are reaching their students. They share their practices with peers to get feedback. They examine student data. They just don't look at it, they *think* about it, and then *take action* to try something different to improve the outcomes reflected in the data. They ask others for feedback. They look at what their students are learning and what they are struggling with to guide the next steps. They have an expert knowledge of where they need to take their students and constantly look at what their children are learning to revise their course of action. When teaching and learning is viewed as a reflective practice of continuous improvement, the cycle begins with vision, followed by instruction, assessment, and reflection.

Reflection happens when educators are alone thinking about their work, but it also happens in small groups or one-on-one when talking about their work. The connection of reflection in the act of teaching is best stated by Joelle Jay (2003) in her book, *Quality Teaching:*

> Reflective teachers face the challenge of truly seeing themselves and their teaching. They approach their practice with openness, wholeheartedness, and responsibility, looking for the better path to take, the edges that need to be smoothed, and the changes they need to make in their practice to improve learning for students. This is the heart of quality teaching . . . and we know in the literature on effective education, one message is consistently clear: the most important influence on student learning is quality teaching. (p. 2)

Socrates, Plato, Jesus, and other great teachers down through the centuries used reflection as the staple of their teaching. They asked questions, told stories, and engaged their students by forcing them to reflect on what they said and meant. Reflection sparks creativity.

Reflection is also an element in the art of administration. Administrators need to consider their districts' journeys and courses of bearing in light of the intended future directions. Triangulating from the past through the present to the future is necessary for the safe passage of an administrator's organization. The ability to step away from the activity within a district or school to review and reflect upon the discourse, decisions, and direction will inform the administrator's next moves.

If administrators are able to contemplate the past and the future simultaneously they create an energy from which new ideas may spring. Creativity and innovation will result from the reflective efforts of leaders and followers alike. This may be a solitary activity but it needn't be so. Conversations designed to cause reflective practice can contribute to powerful insights and fresh ways of seeing the relative position of a school or district as it moves through its reform agenda.

Often the pace of our daily lives restricts the time we need to give adequate reflection to our work. Having the discipline to create the time for reflection will pay tremendous dividends as administrators guide their schools through a reform agenda.

THE NEED FOR REFLECTION

Designworks/USA is an innovative company whose clients include such diverse companies as BMW, Adidas, Compaq, Nokia, John Deere, Intel, Peterbuilt, and many more Fortune 500 companies. Former president Henri Fisker, who designed the BMW Z-8 that was featured in the 1999 James Bond film *The World Is Not Enough*, was a firm believer and advocate of the need for time and reflection in creative process. Reflection means taking time to see things in a new light, to pursue new ideas, and let new directions take their course. Excellence cannot be mandated. It must be grown, and sometimes that growth is not visible to the naked eye. Reflection is the gateway to innovation, and innovation breeds excellence.

FACING FACTS AND DOING SOMETHING ABOUT THEM

Insecure leaders base decisions on tradition—"the way we've always done it"—or on opinion, rather than on data. In the early 1900s Henry Ford had a breakthrough discovery with the Model T. He stayed committed to the concept of that car in spite of the fact that the market grew tired of it. By the mid-1920s Ford lost his premier place as the world's greatest automaker. He failed to keep learning. A failure to make a conscious decision about what is measured often results in a lack of effectiveness and achievement. The best groups measure, learn their lessons, adjust, and review (De Pree 1997). The most effective organizations base their decisions on fact, not popular opinion, and they are willing to go to great lengths to make sure they are getting the best information possible. Facing brutal facts and then having the courage and fortitude to do something about those facts is what puts organizations on the high road to change.

Winston Churchill is an example of someone willing to face the brutal facts (Collins 2001). Early in World War II, he created an entirely separate department outside the normal chain of command. He called this department the Statistical Office. The principal function of this department was to feed him the most brutal facts of reality continuously—completely unfiltered. He relied heavily on this unit throughout the war.

Even in the midst of Europe's darkest days when the Nazi Panzers were sweeping across Europe, Churchill went to bed and slept soundly. "I . . . had no need for cheering dreams," he recalled. "Facts are better than dreams" (Collin 2001, p. 667).

THE POWER OF CRITICAL INDICATORS

Critical indicators are the action items most essential for success. Using data to track critical indicators and making them the priority of the operation is a key to breakthrough results. In winning six of eight championships with the Chicago Bulls, and another three with the Los Angeles Lakers, coach Phil Jackson considered the number of passes before shooting the ball to be a critical indicator. He discovered a correlation between the number of passes and shooting percentage. Based upon that data, Jackson employed the use of the triangle offense to encourage increased ball movement and passing, which in turn, would end up in more baskets (Jackson 1995).

In baseball, general manager Billy Beane of the Oakland Athletics popularized the value of on-base (OB) percentage as a critical indicator of success. The most important thing in baseball is scoring runs. It takes runs to win. When it comes to scoring runs, OB percentage is more important than batting averages because OB percentage tracks how successful someone is in reaching base on a regular basis. Batters with good eyes know how to draw walks. Walks won't show up in batting percentages, but they do show up in OB averages. Every successful, result-oriented enterprise has discovered through data reflection their critical indicators. As a result, they leverage their resources to influence the critical indicators that will yield the biggest dividends.

Car dealerships know that salespeople hate to make follow-up phone calls, but they also know that follow-up phone calls to customers who looked at cars is a critical indicator to increased sales. Knowing this, dealerships have created software that will not allow salespeople to enter in new customer names in their database until they have completed their required callbacks.

Interestingly, educational reformer Douglas Reeves (2005) has tracked the use of non-fiction writing as a critical indicator for student achievement. In working with hundreds of schools and districts over the past decade, he has discovered that non-fiction writing—frequency and proficiency—is more closely correlated to reading score improvement and math achievement than any other single measure. Writing is the most complex learning task a student pursues. It involves applying and thinking deeply about the subject matter. Being able to write means a student can think and express what he or she knows.

USING DATA WALLS TO TRACK CRITICAL INDICATORS

In *Accountability for Learning*, Douglas Reeves (2004) reveals the reason why high school reform is at the forefront of the educational conversation. The average high school teacher can rattle off the names of 18-year-old sophomores who have failed dozens of courses again and again because they don't show up or care enough to try. They can also tell you the longer list of names of students who slide by with D's and C's throughout high school because they have learned how to play the game. But these students' D's are often coward F's—failures that no one is willing to name because they are good kids who try, but in the end these students don't have the skills to pass new high school exit exams. They are the previous underground failures that new accountability policies across the country are bringing to the surface. Schools are beginning to use data walls to track education's critical indicators and seek to discover ways to influence those critical indicators.

In many faculty rooms across the country, data walls are replacing distasteful cartoons, out of date safety reminders, and motivational slogan posters. Data walls make public critical information upon which to reflect and act. Staff rooms are great places for data walls because in the space of lunch and breaks, great ideas often surface in the midst of meaningful conversation and dialogue. Douglas Reeves (2004) documents a large 2,700-student high school whose data wall includes the "Opportunity Academy." At-risk students are placed by staff in the Opportunity Academy early in high school or sometimes even before ninth grade. The Opportunity Academy data wall includes the name of every student and the critical indicators the school has determined most vital to high school success.

The critical indicators they've identified are attendance, reading level, writing level, study skills, and the element of "jazz." All of the Opportunity Academy students are listed on the wall. Those with less than 90 percent attendance are printed in red. Students with a reading level of less than ninth grade are printed in red. Writing and study skills performance assessments are scored on a rubric, and any scores lower than Proficient are printed in red. The element of "jazz" represents those things that internally drive each of these students. Jazz represents what gets these students excited about school. It is the quality of experience element that many schools fail to track in their discussions about student success. The jazz column includes things like football, dance club, video games, music interests, extracurricular activities, interests, and hobbies.

Data on the wall is updated every two weeks and is used to drive decisions. At this large school, students "in the red" are not slipping through the cracks. Staff members are aware of the issues and take actions to remedy them. Students will have their schedules changed, obtain tutoring help, get phone calls home, be mentored, double up on needed skill areas—whatever it takes to meet their need to move them out of the "red zone."

QUALITY OF PRODUCT AND EXPERIENCE

Now that the accountability movement is here to stay, public schools can expect to be measured, compared, and judged—for better or worse. However, the Enron scandal taught us that numbers do not tell the whole story, and they can't identify quality very well. In 1999, Enron was the darling of the stock market. They were a Fortune 500 company whose earnings reports were the hot ticket on Wall Street. We know better now. Enron did not have real market value. Their value was simply elaborate smoke and mirrors. They did not have a quality product.

The public today is looking for a quality product from the public school system. They want students who can read, think, and reason at high levels. They want young people who will be responsible citizens and positive contributors to society. They want hard-working, honest role models. The quality of product is the outcome. It is the target.

Parents are looking for a quality product as well, but they care even more about a quality experience. They want their child to be safe at school and respected. They want their child to be accepted, to be a part of the group, and come home with wonderful stories to tell of things they learned and friendships they forged. The average parent is looking for a great experience along with a wonderful product. School leaders must understand and pursue both high levels of product and experience for the students in their charge.

The advent of computers has made the collection of data and the ranking and sorting of children far easier than ever before dreamed possible. Douglas Reeves (2004) talks about a three tier or level accountability system. Tier I is the accountability system already imposed by state departments and the federal government. School districts are required by state departments to report attendance rates, test scores, and a host of other data. This generic data is used to rank and sort. School systems that focus on quality, however, do not stop at the mandatory data. They know that the numbers don't tell the whole story, and they may even tell a misleading one. For that reason, these systems develop their own "Tier II" data to track.

Tier II data is determined by the school and owned by the school. The school determines a few critical indicators their community will focus on to see the difference that is made in quality of product and experience. These Tier II data points can include a variety of indicators, but the intent is the same: pick a few things within the school's control to influence and see what impact those indicators have on the quality that is produced. The indicators can be anything from the number of service projects in the school, to survey result indicators, volunteer hours, number of students returning homework completed, non-fiction writing assigned, read-at-home slips turned in, books read, or harassment reports filed at the school. The choices are endless, but when schools begin to track and impact what is important to their site, quality is improved.

Tier III accountability is one step beyond owning and developing your own critical indicators. Tier III is reflection. Tier III occurs when leaders reflect deeply upon the data, then change, and paint pictures for others that inspire action. Tier III reflection is most effectively expressed in narrative form by those who are analyzing and acting upon the data.

THE CLEAR LEADER

School systems are steeped in tradition. Good leaders resist the momentum of tradition and look for ways to move the status quo through data. Great leaders go one step further. They reflect deeply upon data and determine their priorities. They are compelled by the future, and are constantly looking for a better tomorrow.

Marcus Buckingham has spent nearly 20 years researching the world's best leaders and managers. His findings resulted in two best selling books: *First Break All the Rules* and *Now, Discover Your Strengths*. After that he went one step further. He wanted to find out the vividness of excellence—the one universal element that truly made leaders successful. He discovered that element was clarity (Breen 2005). Improvement requires change. Change causes anxiety. Great leaders wade through change to arrive at improvement, and they do it through the vessel of clarity. "Clarity is the preoccupation of the effective leader" (p. 65). Leaders that inspire followership through the rough waters of change do so by inspiring a clear vision of the future. They mine all of their data and find the most salient point. They determine the one element their company will focus on and track the data they need to impact that one element most significantly.

Brad Anderson, the CEO of Best Buy, determined that the most important element of his company's success was the quality of the employees in his stores. His vision was clear, and he acted upon it by determining to have the best selected, trained, and equipped employees in the industry. He believed and convinced his people that if their frontline people were better, they would win. Once he determined his priority, he discovered a way to measure it with twelve simple questions. These twelve questions became Best Buy's scoreboard for success (Breen 2005). In the world of data overload, Anderson used the power of reflection to determine what information was most valuable, and he used that information to drive overall success for his company.

Advertising agencies survive on market trends. Rishad Tobaccowala used this same strategy of data reflection to rise to the top of Leo Burnett, a mammoth Chicago advertising agency. Rishad made himself indispensable to his company by becoming an Information Master. He did this by screening all of the data that came his way against a select few yardsticks—critical indicators—and looking for contradictions. His ability to see market trends before they became trends was simply an outcome of his ability to reflect on the data that was presented to him each day.

CONCLUSION: MOVING FROM TRADITION TO DATA TO REFLECTION

Schools have long traditions, and in most cases those traditions hinder change and improvement. Moving beyond tradition begins by taking honest looks at a variety of data inputs, but it doesn't stop there. Priority leaders reflect on the data and generate a clear sense of direction and call to action so that improvement will occur. They are keen to determine the indicators critical to their success, and as they track progress with toward those indicators, they are able to achieve breakthrough results.

10

FROM ARRIVAL TO GROWTH

*For the poet the credo or doctrine is not the point of arrival but is,
on the contrary, the point of departure for the metaphysical journey.*

Joseph Brodsky

Effective change agents cultivate learning and discipline. They are disciplined about learning and resist the feeling of arrival. New learning overcomes the feeling of arrival. When a leader thinks there is nothing left to improve, the organization is doomed to the status quo or a regression from it. The leaders of tomorrow grew up with their computers constantly improving every few years, and they understand there is always room for improvement and thus change. In the technology industry, the sense of arrival brings certain doom to the company because there is a marked departure from the focus on improvement.

THE GREAT ARRIVAL OF THE 2004 RED SOX

One of the greatest stories of arrival in the world of sports occurred in the fall of 2004. The Boston Red Sox arrived. They accomplished something magical. For the first time in 86 years, they won the World Series.

Their journey was not an easy one, and no one really understood how much it meant to "Red Sox Nation" until after the fact. An article in *Sports Illustrated* documented the overwhelming response of the Red Sox arrival in an issue published immediately after the victory. People sent in thousands and thousands of e-mails thanking the Red Sox for winning. Red Sox Nation spans geographic boundaries, political affiliations, and religion. Some people jumped on the bandwagon simply because the little sox were taking on the evil empire—those perennial winners, the New York Yankees. And some say sports is *just a game,* but when the world is a scary place, people need games—forms of entertainment to give them something to look forward to—even to live for.

Lifelong Sox fan, Fred Hale, age 113, of Syracuse, New York, was just such a person. When the Sox won in 2004, he was the oldest man in the United States—older than Babe Ruth himself. Virginia Muise, age 111, of New Hampshire, was the oldest woman in New England. She was a lifelong fan as well. Hale and Muise both died within weeks of the Sox victory. Sometimes just waiting for arrival is a great event, and great arrivals deserve a celebration—but then what? What happens after you arrive? What is next for the Red Sox or the New England Patriots, who in 2004 won their third Super Bowl in four years, or the Chicago Bulls in the heyday of their six championships in 8 years? No matter how good a team does in any given year, there is always next year. In the game of arrival, success can be a stumbling block because it hinders growth.

Outstanding leaders understand that growth is the priority, not arrival, and there is always room for growth. There is always another season; another school year; another class; another book to write; another movie to be made. On growth's journey, taking time to stop, rest, and celebrate milestones of achievement is appropriate, but taking too much time allows the future to pass by. The future is in growth, not arrival.

PERFORMANCE MEASUREMENT: GROWTH IS THE TARGET

At Southwest Airlines, the purpose of performance measurement is to learn and improve over time—not accountability (Gittell 2003). When employees know that measurement equals growth rather than punishment, it frees up workers to take risks and to look at detailed measurement as an ally, rather than a club. A view that links measurement to growth removes the fear factor, and the result is self-motivation. Deming (1986) was clear to point out that fear is a poor long-term motivator. In environments shrouded with fear, people do not take risks. They do not share information. They do not ask for help. There is no trust. There is a lack of morale. Workers become isolated, and the result is a lack of performance. When detailed measurement leads to criticism and fault-finding, measurement is viewed as a negative element. Performance measurement should always be connected with growth and improvement.

Many of the typical performance measurement systems undermine improvement because they weaken the relationships that require cooperation for the organization to improve. If leaders trust their people, and the people trust their leaders, the organization will operate without the element of fear (Gittell 2003). The need for a detailed performance measurement system will also be greatly reduced.

THE MESSY SIDE OF SCHOOL AND DISTRICT IMPROVEMENT

When we engage in linear models of program improvement we tend to set levels, stages, or goals that are met on our way to a destination. Arriving at our destination we idle in the status quo for a while or, on occasion, we immediately move to the next project to continue our improvement. The next project also has its stages and an end point. This buildup followed by a sense of arrival depletes energy levels and casts doubt on our capacity to ever finish with something. Improvement seems like extra effort. It is not a regular part of a school district's routine. It would be wrong to assume that there is an end to improvement in the first place. If there is no end, why then should we think that we have arrived? Yet, this is the prevailing view of school and district improvement. We are okay where we are until we sense a need to get better at which time we make an extra effort to improve and then lapse back into an extended status quo period where our efforts preserve a static or suspended condition thereby avoiding the need to continue the extra effort. This false sense of accomplishment is described here as arrival at a predetermined outcome. In fact, the desired condition for a school is to maintain a constant state of improve-ment, or disequilibrium, as a matter of course.

The concept of arrival inherently signals a stopping point or terminal ending while growth signals movement. When we feel like we've arrived, we actually begin to fall away from our improvements. If we come to a stop then those who are continuing to improve move away from us. We must realize that stopping is actually an act of falling away from im-provement. The effect is much the same as a train arriving at a station where we disembark, and the train pulls away leaving us behind. Such is the experience of school improvement. We ride for a ways only to dis-embark and wait for the next train while the first moves on ahead of us. Many times the second train ends up taking us in another direction alto-gether. As a result, we move periodically but never really get anywhere.

THE LOST MONOPOLY OF PUBLIC EDUCATION

Public education has lost its monopoly in the field. There are home schools, private schools, charter schools, vouchers, and online learning opportunities. We have held fast to traditional delivery systems for too long and other alternatives have overtaken us. Public education arrived decades ago and hasn't significantly moved since. Other forms of edu-cational organizations have grown as alternatives to the extent that pub-lic education's opportunities have been reduced. This phenomenon il-lustrates the error of "arriving" and the failure to grow with the changing dynamics of education in the United States. A further illustration of the point is made by the fact that leaders in the field of education have lost their standing to politicians and business executives. The past decade has seen a proliferation of law requiring educators to strive for im-provement. The field of education has been challenged relentlessly to operate like a business. Taxpayers are disgruntled, legislators are frus-trated, and businesses fear for our country's competitive edge. This is all because public education's earlier monopoly has been taken for granted by its leaders. The consequence was to surrender to the feeling that public education had arrived only to be surpassed by other innovations and ways of providing education. Had the system continued to grow it would not be experiencing the degree of criticism that it does today by those who recognize the stagnation.

MOVING TOWARD A CONTINUOUS GROWTH MODEL

Flexibility, nimbleness, and resilience are attributes of a system that is engaged in continuous improvement and progress. Reaching levels of accomplishment and resting on our laurels creates a perception that we have completed something. If we treat a school as a living system then striving for a healthy and vital learning environment will not have an arbitrary end in the order of events that make up the daily operations. Ends are more easily associated with mechanistic approaches to the business of schooling.

Flexibility, nimbleness, and resilience are attributes of a living system. Considering every accomplishment as a point of departure rather than arrival develops them even further and creates an environment of growth and expansion. The attributes of a living system are important for schools inasmuch as they represent a state of being where the school community is constantly seeking improvements. A striving is felt within the staff and administration that promotes growth in the performance of the school and its learners. This becomes an ever-present condition of the school's climate. Many schools operate out of the perspective of maintaining the status quo and only adjusting as necessary. As a result, when adjustments are completed a sense of arrival is experienced and the reaction to that sense of arrival is to conform to the new status quo and preserve it. Resilience is lost. There is no stretch in a system that places a high value on preserving the status quo. Stretching out toward new ways of doing business conditions the school for changes that improve the environment for teachers and students. Furthermore, if schools only change when required, then they lose the qualities of nimbleness and flexibility that let them identify means for improvement and react quickly to take advantage of the opportunities. The status quo is a school's version of a couch potato. The advise to a couch potato is to become physically fit. A regimen of exercise and diet are usually prescribed. The parallel for schools is to become more flexible, nimble, and resilient.

FLEXIBILITY LEADS TO GROWTH

In the physical sense flexibility increases efficiency and performance. Flexibility allows a body to move further, use less energy, and avoid injury.

It also aids circulation to the joints and increases a body's coordination. Schools are more flexible when they can increase the quality and quantity of their communication, which is the lifeblood of the system. They are also more flexible when staff members are stretching to find new and improved ways to instruct students and organize programs. The combination of communication and stretching creates a synergized coordination that has powerful impacts on the school as a living system. Ultimately, flexibility must be attained in a constructive way so that the system isn't injured in its striving. Even so, flexibility cannot be ignored; it must be developed more fully for the school to benefit. There is greater freedom to act where greater flexibility is attained.

"Jack be nimble, Jack be quick" is the initial line in a popular children's rhyme. Nimbleness was valued for Jack so that he could jump the candlestick. If we are to succeed at jumping over barriers in our schools then we must be nimble. If we are nimble, we can secure opportunities when they present themselves. We can adjust our strategies efficiently and effectively in accordance with issues as they emerge. Finally, nimbleness aids us in confronting the complexities of school environments and all of the things we must consider when improving the system. Nimbleness enables us to strive for a greater good than the status quo.

RESILIENCE AS A BY-PRODUCT OF GROWTH

Resilience is the capacity to "get back up" when we have suffered short-term delays or setbacks. Naturally, if we are risking efforts to improve our schools we will encounter failure and disappointments. If we can increase the collective resilience of the staff then we can better respond when things don't go our way. Resilience is increased when we are nurturing in our relationships and affording participation in our decision-making. If we are to be confident and competent we must grow in our capacity to adapt in the tough times. Resilience is a practiced attribute of a living school system. The interactions of the members of the system must encourage its development. Activities that enable this development include opportunities for the meaningful participation of all members of the organization including opportunities to participate in the evaluation of the system's progress toward improvement. Daily activities are conducted through caring and supportive relationships. Reflective thinking among the members is encouraged. Each individual holds high expectations for the performance of the group's members. Improvement must necessarily create levels of uncertainty as changes are made. The resilience of the staff to endure these changes and the uncertainties they bring is critical to the improvement itself.

When developed fully, the attributes of flexibility, nimbleness, and resilience enable the system to get up from its status quo and move consistently toward improvement for the benefit of the students. Every day represents a new status quo from which we must rise up and move forward. This requires a change in our thinking such that we haven't arrived but are, in fact, just departing.

THE GOAL OF DEPARTURE

Trains, planes, and cars slow down to arrive and speed up to depart. It is imperative that we adjust our thinking to view every day, event, or opportunity as a point of departure or growth. Things accomplished need to be things behind us as we press ever onward toward a better tomorrow. The concept of pressing onward is the human body's state of exercise. In the corporate body it is the continual growth or improvement of the system. Each day provides a new opportunity to advance the system, not to simply preserve the status quo.

What does it mean for organizations to grow? Growth of mature organizations like public schools is not linear even though growth should be continuous. It is better described as cyclical. School district leaders need to continually ask, "Where do we go from here?" This is a conscious effort to review the pathway by which the school has developed and then determine a direction for the immediate future. This effort involves a check of the school's underlying values and principles and the behaviors that influence them. The conclusions that are drawn from such a review can be translated into a new focus, strategy or priority that seizes opportunities for growth. This can be an uncomfortable time for a school because it is the point of breaking away from the known toward another unknown set of circumstances and conditions from which the status quo protects. This is a critical time for a growing organization because failure to push through to the new only leaves the old. That is the point at which we have either arrived or are just departing.

As time progresses, staff members are able to make greater connections and applications of the new opportunity and then growth is accelerated. Growth spurts are followed by periods of refining just prior to the repeating of the entire cycle. Depending upon the focus, strategy, or priority, more than one cycle can be operating at a given time.

IMPROVEMENT SPIKES

Growth in the human body is not linear. A person does not gain the same number of millimeters per day. Growth in humans is sporadic. It is unpredictable. It has patterns, but those patterns are not easily identified. Growth in organizations is similar. Like a living organism, a school system is complex and unpredictable. Improving schools does not happen in a linear fashion. Sometimes growth spikes can be attributed to certain key events, experiences, teaching practices, or policy but not always. Sometimes the growth seems inexplicable, but there is usually an underlying reason. We just haven't dug far enough to find it. Paying attention to critical indicators is one way we can ensure growth. Charted over time improvement spikes begin to flatten out. We can draw a straight line from A to B, but that doesn't mean the journey was linear.

PROFESSIONAL DEVELOPMENT AS GROWTH

Every school district has standards for teaching. Thousands upon thousands of teachers across America are assessed and evaluated every year by these standards and deemed proficient or deficient. The evaluation of teaching staff is one of the chief tasks of an administrator. However, most evaluation systems are not geared toward growth. They are designed for arrival. Teachers either meet the standards or they do not, and if they do, they have arrived. They are equipped to teach. Forward thinking districts are moving away from this arrival mentality when it comes to teaching and learning.

Everyone knows that there is always room for improvement in the complex art of teaching and learning. Educators in Lebanon developed the Professional Growth and Accountability (PG&A) System over a several year time period to reflect this knowledge. A committee was formed with administrative, teaching, and consulting staff members and charged with developing an evaluation system that created an accountability floor but also a growth ceiling so that the feeling of arrival would not exist.

In keeping with the philosophy of continuous improvement, after the group developed the system they were brought back after implementation to refine and improve it. One of the biggest areas needing improvement was developing the growth side of evaluation. In the Lebanon system when teachers demonstrate proficiency in all standards, they are placed on a 4-year growth cycle. Unfortunately, the growth cycle became a "coast" cycle because teacher involvement wasn't formalized, and we learned an important lesson about growth. It doesn't necessarily occur naturally. There must be effort and direction. Gardens do not flourish without planting, watering, and weeding.

In the PG&A revision, growth became formalized. Teachers scoring proficient and above on all standards are now required to join one of several critical friends groups (CFGs) that focuses on a variety of topics related to teaching and learning. Teachers have the liberty and responsibility to chose from a variety of different growth opportunities. Creating an expectation and roadway for growth was a big step toward greater teaching quality throughout all of the schools, and it enabled busy administrators to place their proficient teachers on trajectories of growth so that they could spend the time necessary to help their developing teachers reach proficient levels of performance.

Priority leaders always focus on growth. They look for soft spots in their organization where people are drifting in the current of arrival and adjust the system so that growth becomes the priority. The danger of a growth focus is that workers might feel like they are never good enough and always underperforming. To prevent the feeling of insecurity that comes from continual striving, priority leaders take time to recognize and celebrate benchmark achievements. In this way, workers can catch their breath and high five their colleagues while they prepare to meet the next challenge.

CONCLUSION: LIBERTY IN THE WORKPLACE— THE ULTIMATE BENCHMARK FOR GROWTH

The contest, for ages, has been to rescue Liberty from the grasp of executive power.

Daniel Webster

We hold these truths to be self-evident, that all men are created equal, that they are endowed by their Creator with certain unalienable rights, that among these are life, liberty, and the pursuit of happiness.

Constitution of the United States

Four score and seven years ago our fathers brought forth on this continent, a new nation, conceived in Liberty, and dedicated to the proposition that all men are created equal.

Abraham Lincoln

I know not what course others may take; but as for me, give me liberty, or give me death.

Patrick Henry

A nation conceived in liberty must weave liberty throughout its social fabric. It is our common understanding that each individual shall have the right to think what she or he will and to express openly those thoughts and even to act upon them so long as the action injures no one. The more difficult question is to ask how this individual liberty can weave its way into a corporate body. If we believe that liberty is something given or bestowed upon us by the government, our employer, or our union, then surely we demean the concept of liberty and all those who sacrificed that we might enjoy its benefits.

When addressing the New York Press Club in 1912, President Woodrow Wilson noted, "Liberty has never come from government. Liberty has always come from the subjects of government. The history of government is the history of resistance. The history of liberty is the history of the limitation of government, not the increase of it."

We necessarily employ governing structures in our institutions including our public school systems. It is here that we rest on the horns of a dilemma. It is by our need to create order and direction within a system that we often tread upon the liberty necessary for our employees to freely participate with ownership in the mission of the system. Schools can be no greater than the belief we hold for individual liberty. When constraints are placed upon liberty within the workplace, whether by employers or unions, the outcome is, at best, diminished productivity, but more frequently it is dissention and other counterproductive actions. Typically, the final outcome is increased policy and added rules.

Daniel Webster, in a speech to the United States Senate, noted: "The contest, for ages, has been to rescue Liberty from the grasp of executive power." Today's leadership literature continues to illustrate Webster's point as readers are supplied with tips to motivate, evaluate, and communicate with the workforce almost always with the intention of keeping order within the organization.

So often, employers hear complacency in the workers who say, "Just tell me what to do and I'll do it." Employees are not necessarily inclined to exercise their liberty because they perceive it as unwanted behavior or they shy from the responsibility that it brings. President Wilson makes the point: "I believe in human liberty as I believe in the wine of life. There is no salvation for men in the pitiful condescension of industrial masters. Guardians have no place in a land of freemen."

So on the one horn we see employers and unions who strive for control to move the organization in the way they would have it go while on the other horn are employees who are complacent or resistant to the practice of liberty in the workplace. Thomas Jefferson has written, "I would rather be exposed to the inconveniences attending too much liberty than those attending too small a degree of it."

Employers utilize time-honored methods to manage their organizations. They plan, set goals, develop policies, and problem-solve. These activities tend to establish conformity and restrict liberty. Alternatively, visioning, establishing priorities, seeking opportunities, developing capacity in others and creating community may provide space for the exercise of liberty within the organization. The more controlling you are in your leadership and the less empowering, the more you restrict liberty, and without liberty, there are low levels of responsibility and ownership.

Liberty comes with a price. Liberty in management instills confidence, confronts differences of opinion, creates resilience, bestows confidence, and builds capacity. It enables us to truly grow and move forward with continuous progress. Liberty is suppressed by packed agendas. Time must be given for discussion, conversation, and to work through issues in relationship with others. Priority leadership liberates. Priority leadership begins with a vision, is supported by priorities, and sparked by pursuing targets of opportunity. The liberated leader knows how important it is to operate from a vision rather than a plan. Liberated leaders are confident. They are willing to take risks and engage in hard conversations. They reject the status quo, are liberated to act, and yet at that the same time they are accountable for their actions.

The slaves were freed in 1862 by policy. Martin Luther King Jr. liberated African Americans in 1962 by determined actions. Policy can free, but it cannot liberate. Contracts free, but they do not liberate. Without intellectual liberty, there is only freedom. In Russia under Communism, there was freedom—citizens were not interned, but there was no liberty, which is the ability to think and act and be self-determinate.

The delegation of authority is the creation of the opportunity for liberty to emerge. Freedom and liberty are not the same. Freedom removes boundaries. Liberty is the actions of the freed. Liberty is tarrying because our society allows us to cast blame. Each of us possesses the freedom to determine whether we will or will not be liberated. In the workplace we are free, but we are not liberated. Liberty is a level of engagement. It is intrinsic. It is the ability to act upon your beliefs. Liberty gathers energy and creates a following. It is the by-product of growth.

In moving from arrival to growth, we must enter into levels of systemic change: renewal, reform, and restructuring (Conley 1999). Renewal activities improve the system in small ways, and reform is policy that must be implemented, but restructuring gets at the heart of systemic change. Restructuring is only successful when the workers become intrinsically motivated to change and improve. Teaching staffs cannot restructure without invoking elements of liberty. All staff members need to be liberated, not just teachers, but secretaries, support staff, and students as well. The liberated spirit constantly seeks for improvement in all areas. What would schools look like if all teachers were liberated, all staff members, and all students? Workers prefer the status quo because it is known, and change is uncomfortable. A liberated staff will make sure the change agenda moves forward, or they will overthrow the leader. The growth of priority leadership will create liberty in the workplace.

APPENDIX:
PRIORITY LEADER ASSESSMENT

Operating as a Priority Leader is a complex, ongoing process. Old habits die hard, and many of us were trained in leadership models and styles that are contrary to the continuums presented in this book. We thought it would be helpful to include a tool for assessing leadership growth according to the ten continuums of priority leadership. In this fifty-question assessment, answer each question according to your level of agreement. Once you have completed the assessment, follow the directions to place yourself on the continuums of priority leadership.

It is important to understand that continuums chart growth. We understand that everyone is on a learning journey when it comes to leadership. Understanding the continuums and applying the principles of priority leadership will result in leveraging change and improving achievement in your school district. We are convinced that if you are not seeing the change your organization needs, the first answer is not spending more money on new programs or extra training. A lack of change and improvement is first and foremost a leadership problem. Follow the leader. Analyze the leader's operating methods. When leaders begin thinking and acting as priority leaders, there will be change and improvement in the organization.

Take this assessment at different times to see where you land. Returning to it often will help you understand the key concepts of priority leadership, and as your thinking begins to change, you will find that your actions and those of your followers will change as well. In responding to the questions, try not to "figure out" the right answer. Assessments of this nature are most effective when respondents simply respond with the first thought that comes into their mind.

On a separate piece of paper, answer the following questions according to the following scale:

a = Strongly Agree
b = Agree
c = Agree and Disagree
d = Disagree
e = Strongly Disagree

1) Continuously examining visions and beliefs about the future sets the stage for motivating change and improvement. (PV)

     a   b   c   d   e

2) I do not feel comfortable delegating projects unless I know the person will get it done right. (CB)

     a   b   c   d   e

3) I rely upon my school district's policies to make my decisions. (PTO)

     a   b   c   d   e

4) I am very careful to plan improvements, and I spend so much time developing plans, there is little time or energy left for implementation or reflection. (PV)

     a   b   c   d   e

5) I can state my organization's top priorities. (GP)

     a   b   c   d   e

6) I engage in one-on-one conversations with my supervisor on a regular basis. (AL)

     a   b   c   d   e

7) New leaders from outside the organization are the most effective when it comes to continuous improvement because they are not afraid to make sweeping changes. (SR)

   a   b   c   d   e

8) The most effective leaders focus primarily on improving the weaknesses of their staff members. (SL)

   a   b   c   d   e

9) In high functioning communities, everyone will feel responsible when a problem exists, and they will jump in to fix it. (CB)

   a   b   c   d   e

10) I am quick to accept responsibility—even for things that are not my fault—rather than place blame on others. (SR)

   a   b   c   d   e

11) A high level of compliance is necessary for success. (SL)

   a   b   c   d   e

12) I regularly read books and articles about education and how to improve it. (AG)

   a   b   c   d   e

13) In my school district, student performance data drives our decisions. (TDR)

   a   b   c   d   e

14) I provide choices and options to my staff to help encourage internally motivated behavior. (CP)

   a   b   c   d   e

15) You cannot influence community. It either exists or does not exist. (CB)

   a   b   c   d   e

16) The people that I work with are intrinsically motivated. (GP)

   a   b   c   d   e

17) Admitting mistakes is central to building relationships with others. (SR)

    a   b   c   d   e

18) I spend a lot of time in conversations that greatly influence the actions I take. (AL)

    a   b   c   d   e

19) I have a list of at-risk students in my office and know the interventions we are using with these students. (TDR)

    a   b   c   d   e

20) It is best in the long run not to stir up conflict and potentially hurt people's feelings. (CP)

    a   b   c   d   e

21) The most effective visions are not developed in isolation. They are developed by the collective whole. (PV)

    a   b   c   d   e

22) You will get better results by pursuing opportunities for improvement rather than following established policies and guidelines. (PTO)

    a   b   c   d   e

23) People need clear guidelines in order to achieve the desired end result. (SL)

    a   b   c   d   e

24) I spend a lot of time defending/convincing others of my ideas. (AL)

    a   b   c   d   e

25) Managing disagreement is critical to achieving high levels of performance. (CP)

    a   b   c   d   e

26) To become a talented leader, you must focus on your strengths. (SL)

    a   b   c   d   e

27) Relationships and teamwork are central to achieving quality of product and experience. (SR)

  a   b   c   d   e

28) Improvement is mostly incremental. (AG)

  a   b   c   d   e

29) Reflection is central to innovation. (TDR)

  a   b   c   d   e

30) Workers will take advantage of you if you provide them lots of choices and options. (CP)

  a   b   c   d   e

31) Staff empowerment is a critical ingredient to improved performance. (SL)

  a   b   c   d   e

32) The leader is responsible for building capacity in his/her followers. (CB)

  a   b   c   d   e

33) Making rules and policies generally create more problems than they solve. (PTO)

  a   b   c   d   e

34) Most planning documents are not referred to or consulted after they are written. (PV)

  a   b   c   d   e

35) Effective leaders always delegate. If someone can't resolve it, you can help them with it later. (CB)

  a   b   c   d   e

36) Effective leadership begins with effective management. (GP)

  a   b   c   d   e

37) The average worker doesn't have the capacity or ability to solve complex problems, and that is why there is a such a need for talented, experienced, wise, and well-trained leaders. (SR)

    a   b   c   d   e

38) Collective wisdom is in the group. The answer is usually in the room. (AL)

    a   b   c   d   e

39) Tomorrow's success is built from the rubble of today's failure. (AG)

    a   b   c   d   e

40) Our staff meetings are so crammed with stuff to do that there is little time for meaningful reflection and dialog. (TDR)

    a   b   c   d   e

41) I don't say what I am thinking because I don't want to be rejected by my boss or other leaders. (CP)

    a   b   c   d   e

42) I am responsible for my learning and pursue learning experiences via conferences, reading, writing, and meeting with others on a regular basis. (AL)

    a   b   c   d   e

43) I would rather fail doing something new than not to take the risks for fear of failure. (PTO)

    a   b   c   d   e

44) I am comfortable without knowing all the answers. (GP)

    a   b   c   d   e

45) Deep, meaningful change is not possible without a strong vision. (PV)

    a   b   c   d   e

46) I am always looking for a new opportunity for growth. (AG)

    a   b   c   d   e

47) Our school and district make adjustments to our actions based upon constantly reviewing data. (TDR)

    a   b   c   d   e

48) Innovation requires you to look and work outside of the box. (PTO)

    a   b   c   d   e

49) Priorities should be revised once they have been established. (GP)

    a   b   c   d   e

50) Success can be a threat to growth. (AG)

    a   b   c   d   e

APPENDIX ANSWERS

Based on how you answered the 50 questions, score your responses according to the following guidelines. It is a good idea to photocopy the answer sheet so you can use it more than once. The range for each continuum is from 5 to 25 points, and it is designed as a way to chart growth in the concepts over time. There are many ways to use this assessment, and we are very interested in learning how helpful the tool is and how you or your organization is using it. Please send your stories and experiences to: robhess@comcast.net. We are also available to conduct a variety of workshops and training sessions about priority leadership. We are convinced that applying these concepts over time will embed systemic growth and improvement in your organization.

PV: From Planning to Vision

1: _____ (a = 5; b = 4; c = 3; d = 2; e = 1)
4: _____ (e = 5; d = 4; c = 3; b = 2; a = 1)

21: _____ (a = 5; b = 4; c = 3; d = 2; e = 1)
34: _____ (a = 5; b = 4; c = 3; d = 2; e = 1)
45: _____ (a = 5; b = 4; c = 3; d = 2; e = 1)

Chapter 1: From Planning to Vision total: _____

GP: From Goals to Priorities

5: _____ (a = 5; b = 4; c = 3; d = 2; e = 1)
16: _____ (a = 5; b = 4; c = 3; d = 2; e = 1)
36: _____ (a = 5; b = 4; c = 3; d = 2; e = 1)
44: _____ (a = 5; b = 4; c = 3; d = 2; e = 1)
49: _____ (e = 5; d = 4; c = 3; b = 2; a = 1)

Chapter 2: From Goals to Priorities total: _____

PTO: From Policy to Targets of Opportunity

3: _____ (c = 5; d = 4; b = 3; e = 2; a = 1)
22: _____ (a = 5; b = 4; c = 3; d = 2; e = 1)
33: _____ (a = 5; b = 4; c = 3; d = 2; e = 1)
43: _____ (a = 5; b = 4; c = 3; d = 2; e = 1)
48: _____ (a = 5; b = 4; c = 3; d = 2; e = 1)

Chapter 3: From Policy to Targets of Opportunity total: _____

CB: From Problem-Solving to Capacity-Building

2: _____ (e = 5; d = 4; c = 3; b = 2; a = 1)
9: _____ (a = 5; b = 4; c = 3; d = 2; e = 1)
15: _____ (e = 5; d = 4; c = 3; b = 2; a = 1)
32: _____ (a = 5; b = 4; c = 3; d = 2; e = 1)
35: _____ (a = 5; b = 4; c = 3; d = 2; e = 1)

Chapter 4: From Problem-Solving to Capacity-Building total: _____

SR: From Fear of Separation to Relationships and Teamwork

7: _____ (d = 5; e = 4; c = 3; b = 2; a = 1)
10: _____ (a = 5; b = 4; c = 3; d = 2; e = 1)

17: _____ (a = 5; b = 4; c = 3; d = 2; e = 1)
27: _____ (a = 5; b = 4; c = 3; d = 2; e = 1)
37: _____ (e = 5; d = 4; c = 3; b = 2; a = 1)

Chapter 5: From Fear of Separation to Relationships and Teamwork total: _____

SL: From Controlled Management to Shared Leadership

8: _____ (e = 5; d = 4; c = 3; b = 2; a = 1)
11: _____ (e = 5; d = 4; c = 3; b = 2; a = 1)
23: _____ (e = 5; d = 4; c = 3; b = 2; a = 1)
26: _____ (a = 5; b = 4; c = 3; d = 2; e = 1)
31: _____ (a = 5; b = 4; c = 3; d = 2; e = 1)

Chapter 6: From Controlled Management to Shared Leadership total: _____

AL: From Hidden Agendas to Authentic Listening

6: _____ (a = 5; b = 4; c = 3; d = 2; e = 1)
18: _____ (a = 5; b = 4; c = 3; d = 2; e = 1)
24: _____ (e = 5; d = 4; c = 3; b = 2; a = 1)
38: _____ (a = 5; b = 4; c = 3; d = 2; e = 1)
42: _____ (a = 5; b = 4; c = 3; d = 2; e = 1)

Chapter 7: From Hidden Agendas to Authentic Listening total: _____

CP: From Conformance to Performance

14: _____ (a = 5; b = 4; c = 3; d = 2; e = 1)
20: _____ (e = 5; d = 4; c = 3; b = 2; a = 1)
25: _____ (a = 5; b = 4; c = 3; d = 2; e = 1)
30: _____ (e = 5; d = 4; c = 3; b = 2; a = 1)
41: _____ (e = 5; d = 4; c = 3; b = 2; a = 1)

Chapter 8: From Conformance to Performance total: _____

TDR: From Tradition to Data to Reflection

13: _____ (b = 5; a = 4; c = 3; d = 2; e = 1)
19: _____ (a = 5; b = 4; c = 3; d = 2; e = 1)
29: _____ (a = 5; b = 4; c = 3; d = 2; e = 1)
40: _____ (e = 5; d = 4; c = 3; b = 2; a = 1)
47: _____ (a = 5; b = 4; c = 3; d = 2; e = 1)

Chapter 9: From Tradition to Data to Reflection total: _____

AG: From Arrival to Growth

12: _____ (a = 5; b = 4; c = 3; d = 2; e = 1)
28: _____ (e = 5; d = 4; c = 3; b = 2; a = 1)
39: _____ (a = 5; b = 4; c = 3; d = 2; e = 1)
46: _____ (a = 5; b = 4; c = 3; d = 2; e = 1)
50: _____ (b = 5; a = 4; c = 3; d = 2; e = 1)

Chapter 10: From Arrival to Growth total: _____

Add up the total for each continuum to discover your overall priority leadership score.

Overall score: _____

0–50	Dictator
51–100	Manager
101–150	Planner
151–200	Stategist
201–250	Priority Leader

REFERENCES

AATH. 2004. "The Association for Applied and Therapeutic Humor." Retrieved January 8, 2005, from www.aath.org.

Anders, G. 2002, March. "How Intel Puts Innovation Inside." *Fast Company* 56: 122.

Bambino, D. 2002, March. "Critical Friends." *Educational Leadership* 59, no. 6: 25–27.

Barr, R. D., and W. H. Parrett. 2003. *Saving Our Students, Saving Our Schools: 50 Proven Strategies for Revitalizing At-risk Students and Low-performing Schools.* Thousand Oaks, Calif.: Corwin Press.

Barth, R. 2001. *Learning by Heart.* San Francisco: Jossey-Bass.

Betances, S. 2002, June. Keynote speech, Confederation of Oregon School Administrators conference. Seaside, Ore.

Bottoms, G. 2001. "Leadership Matters: Building Leadership Capacity." Southern Regional Education Board. Atlanta, Ga. Retrieved from www.sreb.org.

Breen, B. 2005, March. "The Clear Leader." *Fast Company* 92.

Buckingham, M., and C. Coffman. 1999. *First Break All the Rules: What the World's Greatest Managers Do Differently.* New York: Simon and Schuster.

Byrne, J. 2004, April. "Practicing More Than Jack Preached." *Fast Company* 81.

Camelleri, Vanessa, and Anthony Jackson. 2005, March. "Nurturing Excellence Through the Arts." *Educational Leadership* 62, no. 6: 60–64.

Collins, J. 2001. *Good to Great.* New York: Harper Business.

Conley, D. T. 1999. *Roadmap to Restructuring: Charting the Course of Change in American Education.* 2nd ed. University of Oregon: Eric Clearinghouse on Educational Management.

Danielson, C. 1996. *Enhancing Professional Practice: A Framework for Teaching.* Alexandria, Va.: ASCD.

Decter, M. 1971. *The Liberated Woman and Other Americans.* New York: Coward-McCann.

Deming, W. E. 1986. *Out of the Crisis.* Cambridge: Massachusetts Institute of Technology Press.

De Pree, M. 1997. *Leading without Power: Finding Hope in Serving Community.* San Francisco: Jossey-Bass.

DuFour, R. 2003, Winter. "Leading Edge." *Journal of Staff Development* 24, no. 1: 77–78.

Edgar, E. 2005. "Reflections on School Reform and Role of Special Education." Paper presented at the Oregon Conference 2005. Eugene: February 25, 2005.

Elmore, R. F., and D. Burney. 1999. Pp. 266–71 in L. Darling-Hammond and G. Sykes, eds., *Teaching as the Learning Profession: Handbook of Policy and Practice.* San Francisco: Jossey-Bass.

Gillon, S. M. 2000. *"That's Not What We Meant To Do": Reform and Its Unintended Consequences in Twentieth-Century America.* New York: Norton.

Gittell, J. H. 2003. *The Southwest Way: Using the Power of Relationships to Achieve High Performance.* New York: McGraw-Hill.

Golly, H., and J. Sprague. 2004. *BEST Behavior: Building Positive Behavior Support in Schools.* Longmount, Colo.: Sopris West.

Harvey, J. 1988. *The Abilene Paradox.* San Francisco: Jossey-Bass.

Healthfield, S. M. *Book Review: Birth of the Chaordic Age.* Retrieved December 19, 2004, from About.com.

Hess, R. T. 2005. *Excellence, Equity, and Efficiency: How Principals and Policymakers Can Survive the Triangle of Tension.* Lanham, Md.: Scarecrow Press.

Hesselbein, F. 2004. *Hesselbein on Leadership.* San Francisco: Jossey-Bass.

Hock, D. 1999. *Birth of the Chaordic Age.* San Francisco: Berrett-Koehler.

Howley, C. B., and H. L. Harmon. 2000. *Small High Schools That Flourish: Rural Context, Case Studies, and Resources.* Washington, D.C.: U.S. Department of Education.

Jackson, P. 1995. *Sacred Hoops: Spiritual Lessons of a Hardwood Warrior.* New York: Hyperion.

Jay, J. K. 2003. *Quality Teaching: Reflection as the Heart of Practice.* Lanham, Md.: Scarecrow Press.

Johnson, J. 2004. "What School Leaders Want." *Educational Leadership* 61, no. 7: 24–27.

Killion, J. P., and G. R. Todnem. 1991. "A Process for Personal Theory Building." *Educational Leadership* 43, no. 6: 14–16.

King, K. 2004. "The Little School that Can't Be Beat." *Sports Illustrated*, August, 23, 2004.

Klein, A. 1988. *The Healing Power of Humor.* New York: Penguin Putnam.

Kouzes, J. M., and B. Z., Posner. 1995. *The Leadership Challenge.* San Francisco: Jossey-Bass.

Krajewski, B. 2005, March. "In Their Own Words." *Educational Leadership* 62, no. 6.

Lagace, M. 2004, July 12. "Enron's Lessons for Managers." *Working Knowledge.* Harvard Business School.

Lencioni, P. M. 2002. *The Five Dysfunctions of a Team: A Leadership Fable.* San Francisco: Jossey-Bass.

Lewis, M. 2003. *Moneyball: The Art of Winning An Unfair Game.* New York: Norton.

Lieberman, A., and L. Miller. 2004. *Teacher Leadership.* San Francisco: Jossey-Bass.

Lindstrom, P. H., and M. Speck. 2004. *The Principal as Professional Development Leader.* Thousand Oaks, Ca.: Corwin.

Littky, D. 2005, February 27. "Big Picture Schools." Paper presented at the National Association of Secondary School Principals Conference, San Francisco.

———. 2004. *The Big Picture.* Alexandria, Va.: Association for Supervision and Curriculum Development.

Marzano, R. J. 2003. *What Works in Schools: Translating Research into Action.* Alexandria, Va.: Association for Supervision and Curriculum Development.

Maxwell Motivation, Inc. 1998. *The 21 Irrefutable Laws of Leadership.* Maxwell, Ga.: Maxwell Motivation, Inc.

Mintzberg, H. 1994. *The Rise and Fall of Strategic Planning.* New York: Free Press.

Nasar, S. 1998. *A Beautiful Mind.* New York: Simon and Schuster.

Norman, D. A. 1998. *The Design of Everyday Things.* New York: Basic Book.

Pascale, R., Millemann, M., and Gioja, L. 2000. *Surfing the Edge of Chaos: The Laws of Nature and the New Laws of Business.* New York: Crown Business.

Reeves, Douglas. 2005, February 27. "Getting Accountability Right." Paper presented at the National Association of Secondary School Principals Conference, San Francisco.

———. 2004. *Accountability for Learning: How Teachers and School Leaders Can Take Charge.* Alexandria, Va.: Association for Supervision and Curriculum Development.

———. 2002. *The Daily Disciplines of Leadership.* San Francisco: Jossey-Bass.

Renzulli, Joseph, Marci Gentry, and Sally Reis. 2004, September. "A Time and Place for Authentic Leadership." *Educational Leadership* 62, no. 1: 73–77.

Robbins, S. 2005, April. "Truth and Trust: They Go Together." *Working Knowledge.* Boston: Harvard Business School.

Roberto, M. 2005. *Why Great Leaders Don't Take Yes for an Answer: Managing for Conflict and Consensus*. Philadelphia: Wharton School Publishing.

Roberts, M. 2001. *Horse Sense for People*. New York: Viking.

Rubin, H. 1999. "Only the Pronoid Survive." *Fast Company* 29: 330.

Salter, M. S. 2003. "Innovation Corrupted: The Rise and Fall of Enron." Harvard Business School. Harvard Business Online, <www.harvardbusinessonline>.

Sample, S. 2002. *The Contrarian's Guide to Leadership*. San Francisco: Jossey-Bass.

Sanders, W. L. 1998, December. "Value-Added Assessment: A Method for Measuring the Effects of the System, School and Teacher on the Rate of Student Academic Progress." *The School Administrator*.

Schmoker, M. 2004, February. "Tipping Point: From Feckless Reform to Substantive Instructional Improvement." *Phi Delta Kappa* 85, no. 6.

———. 1996. *Results: The Key to Continuous School Improvement*. Alexandria, Va.: ASCD.

Schon, D. 1990. *Educating the Reflective Practitioner: Toward a New Design for Teaching and Learning in the Profession*. San Francisco: Jossey-Bass.

———. 1983. *The Reflective Practitioner: How Professionals Think in Action*. Basic Books. New York.

Senge, P. 1994. *The Fifth Discipline Fieldbook*. New York: Doubleday.

Sergiovanni, T. J. 1994. *Building Community in Schools*. San Francisco: Jossey-Bass.

Silver, M. 2005, January 24. "Pat Answer." *Sports Illustrated*, pp. 38–46.

Simpson, J. O. 2003, January. "Beating the Odds." *American School Board Journal* 190, no. 1: 43–47.

Sizer, T. R. 1984. *Horace's Compromise: The Dilemma of the American High School*. Boston: Houghton Mifflin.

Sparks, D. 2005. *Leading for Results*. Thousand Oaks, Calif.: Corwin.

Taylor, W. C. 1999, June. "The Leader of the Future." *Fast Company* 25: 130.

Trout, S. K. 1998. "Humor Touches the Whole Brain—The Whole Person." Paper presented at the National Association for the Education of Young Children conference. Toronto, Canada.

Viorst, J. 1986. *Necessary Losses*. Simon and Schuster: New York.

Waldrop, M. M. 1996, October/November issue. "Dee Hock on Management." *Fast Company* 5: 79.

Webber, A. M. 2002, May. "Are All Consultants Corrupt?" *Fast Company* 58: 130.

Wheatley, M. J. 1999. *Leadership and the New Science: Discovering Order in a Chaotic World*. San Francisco: Berret-Koehler Publishers.

Whitaker, T. 2004. *What Great Teachers Do Differently: Fourteen Things That Matter Most*. Larchmont, N.Y.: Eye on Education.

Zimmerman, P. 2005, January 31. "Dr. Z's Forecast." *Sports Illustrated*, pp. 50–51.

ABOUT THE AUTHORS

DR. ROBERT HESS

Rob has worked in schools for the past 19 years. He spent 10 of those years as a classroom teacher at the high school and middle school levels. He has been a principal and vice principal for 8 years. As an administrator, he has worked at the high school, middle school, and K–8 levels, and his experience has uniquely qualified him as a K–12 educator. His most recent principalship was at Pioneer School in Lebanon, Oregon. Pioneer is a K–8 school of 500 students with 70 percent of the students eligible for free and reduced lunch. During his 3 years at Pioneer, Rob saw his school produce breakthrough results with over 90 percent of all students meeting or exceeding state standards in reading and math. Dr. Hess has learned a great deal about leadership, change, and school improvement through his experiences, and those lessons are reflected in *Priority Leadership.* He is currently the Student Achievement Leader for Springfield School District in Springfield, Oregon. Springfield is the eleventh largest school district in Oregon, and Rob is responsible for assisting the district's twenty-four schools with the vision of school improvement and student achievement.

While working full time he completed a Doctor of Education degree at the University of Oregon in 2003. He has taught graduate level education courses at the University of Oregon, Oregon State, and Lewis &

Clark College. During his career as an administrator, he has conducted several workshops and presentations at state and national level conferences. He has developed a website (www.breakthroughschools.org) to support school improvement and encourage networking among educators. In January 2005 his first book was published by Rowman & Littlefield Education: *Excellence, Equity, and Efficiency: How Principals Can Survive the Triangle of Tension*. His expertise is leadership, systemic change, school improvement, student achievement, and quality through continuous progress. He conducts high quality workshops on these topics and can be reached at: robhess@comcast.net.

DR. JAMES ROBINSON

Jim has worked in the field of education for the past 32 years. He has taught at all levels, kindergarten through postgraduate. He has been a classroom teacher, an instructional specialist, a principal, a curriculum director, and a superintendent. As an agent of change, he has led three different districts through reform agendas that have significantly improved student achievement. His reforms have withstood the most difficult challenge of all—they have endured the test of time by continuing after his departure.

Jim currently serves in Lebanon, Oregon, as superintendent. He has held that office for the past 8 years. He is a pioneer in the concept of priority leadership who constantly looks for targets of opportunity to further the identified causes of the district. His style employs as much top-down leadership as necessary and encourages as much bottom-up ownership as possible.

The Lebanon school district was historically an underperforming system where state achievement greatly outpaced local performance levels when Jim assumed his leadership position 7 years ago. The district now enjoys test scores significantly above state averages in all basic skills areas. Jim is a graduate of Lewis & Clark College (1970). He holds a Master's Degree (1975) and Ph.D. (1980) from the University of Oregon. Jim can be reached at: robinsja@pacific.com.